THE CONQUEST OF LONELINESS

THE
Conquest
OF
Loneliness

BY ERIC P. MOSSE, M.D.

RANDOM HOUSE · NEW YORK

To Marianne

Preface & Acknowledgment

THIS BOOK is written for those who feel lonely—for everybody.

Each branch of science—and psychoanalysis is a science—has its own special lingo. I've tried to avoid using it as much as possible without condescending and without oversimplifying. All too often this lingo has served to hide rather than to clarify the problems of human behavior, and the x-ray of human emotional complexity has been substituted for the picture itself. That which is colorful and brimming with life becomes black and white when reduced to bare psychological terminology. It is for this reason, and to save their human qualities, that I have tried in this book to present case histories, which are commonly written in a style of aseptic sterility, as short stories. Each story is derived from the specific problem of a real patient; if the reader feels that he is being exhibited and exposed in his nudity, it only proves what it is supposed to: there are no singular cases. Similarity between one's own experience and the experience of others merely shows the existence of the pattern.

Although all my patients and all my friends and enemies have helped in forming the concept of this book, my thanks go out especially to Nancy Gross, who has edited and organized the manuscript with great skill, devotion, human understanding and intelligence of her heart. I am also in grateful debt to Alis De Sola, who, in one of those give-and-take conversations, conceived the idea of the book, leaving gracefully to me the toil and sweat of transposing it into reality.

Eric P. Mosse, M.D.

Contents

Contents

The Conquest of Loneliness

Loneliness, far from being a rare and curious phenomenon . . . is the central and inevitable fact of human existence. When we examine the moments, acts and statements of all kind of people—not only the grief and ecstasy of the greatest poets, but also the huge unhappiness of the average soul, as evidenced by the innumerable strident words of abuse, hatred, contempt, mistrust and scorn that forever grate upon our ears as the manswarm passes us in the streets —we find, I think, that they are all suffering from the same thing. The final cause of their complaint is loneliness.

—THOMAS WOLFE
The Anatomy of Loneliness

Introduction

Y OU WERE BORN into an alien world. You were born help-less, with only your suckling instinct to sustain you. From the very moment of your birth, when the rigor and pain of life outside the womb first burst upon your consciousness, you have been, in the deepest biological sense, alone. Yet you were not always so; in the nine idyllic months of your embryonic life you were not isolated, but a parasitic part of another. Then you repeated, in fantastic condensation, millions of years of evolution's trials, errors and triumphs. At birth, you were far more than a miniature human being. Within you, you carry a whole record of the development of life, a continuing story of the aeons bygone since the first blob of protoplasm took food and reproduced itself in some primeval sea.

In your first moments of being as a single fertilized cell, you were close to leading the ideal life of the amoeba. Here is the simplest of existences. To eat, simply flow around food, incorporate what is useful, excrete the rest. To create a new generation, simply divide in the middle. Later, in your embryonic evolution that paralleled so closely the story of life itself, came the gills, another ancestral post-script of your primordial forebears. In you was the tang and tide of the prehistoric oceans, during the millions of years when gills of creatures now fossils strained oxygen from the teeming, saline seas. In you, too, lay something of the time when clumsy amphibious beasts slithered onto sandy beaches and, at last, onto green-carpeted soil, firm earth beneath the exploratory fins that yearned to be feet. And something was left in you of the dramatic emancipation by which front feet became hands that could grasp, by which foamy lungs were developed that could extract oxygen from pure air. Gone was this dependence upon the oxygenated sea. Yet even now, you hold within you the sea and its saga—its foam in your lungs, its salinity in your blood, all its legacy in your very ability to exist on dry land.

The inheritance of all this was perpetuated in your genes. It was bequeathed to you through your parents, your grandparents, your great-grandparents, from those first protozoan specks of life. Your legacy comes not alone from the dim pageant of the past, before man, it comes as well from what the Neanderthals suffered, what the Cro-Magnons enjoyed, from the wild spear-throwing pursuits of the Visigoths, the intellectual eruptions of ancient Greece and the brash experimentation of medieval alchemists. In you, hidden in the pattern you will pass on, lie the drunken unions of bacchanalian nights, the gaping lacerations of dying flesh; lie famine, pestilence, deaths on the bed of childbirth and in the horrors of the battlefield. But not all is ugly and torturous; you also hold the victories of mariners over fog, storm and reef; the smiles of young lovers, their spats and joyous reconciliations.

In short, no matter how alone or lonely you may feel, you contain the mixed blessing of everything and everybody that ever lived. Indeed—and no humor is intended—your troubles did not really begin until you were born and you added to this enormous legacy of evolution the imprint of your own character and individuality.

Although you remember nothing of what befell you before birth, you have an all too real comprehension, if not memory, of your experiences soon thereafter. Sometimes, in confusion and mist of mind, you can retrace the remnants of those early days and nights of alternating fear and joy, especially during the process of modern psychiatric and analytic therapy. As observers, too, you watch and reflect, often with great personal insight and empathy, upon the behavior or, at least, the semaphoric signals, of an infant in its early days, particularly in those months (of which its own recollection will ever be dim) before it acquires the talent of language.

None of the infant's behavior is conscious or "planned." It is dictated by what we call instinct. If it is not something handed down to us by the great compulsion of heredity, neither is it directed by the conscious ego, that mysterious center of our being which develops later in response to the travails and raptures of life itself. The infant suckles because it feels the discomfort of hunger or thirst. Appeased by its full little belly, it feels at peace and falls asleep. Rhythmically, this primitive cycle repeats itself, the endless circle of tension and relief. This ceaseless craving of the infant for surcease of tension survives as one of the basic mechanisms of life. Practically every excretion and secretion—sweat, tears—is the fluid embodiment of such a release. Sweat is a release of the body's reaction to overheating, tears a release of emotions, muscular activity a discharge of pent-up energy. In motion, in the violence of sport, in the consoling fatigue that follows satisfying work, there is a reversion of a sort to that first cycle: hunger—sucking—sleep. This infantile cycle is the roomy cellar of biochemical tension in human beings. From that foundation it evolves into the higher floors, the more complex levels of emotional, physical and psychic life on which man acts out his days.

Aeons of evolution and his biological nature and inheritance make Homo sapiens what he is. The first years of his life as a separate and unique entity, plus the family and the culture into which he is born give each man his distinct personality. Because every man is alone, every man can become lonely. And the dynamics of loneliness can be seen in the ways men behave when they are thrown back and exposed to their earlier sensations of miserable isolation, can be seen in all the familiar and strange, social and antisocial forms human behavior can take.

Part One: The Facts

CHAPTER ONE

In the Cellar: Biology

LONELINESS IS A disease—a disease of the emotions. It is a disease to which everyone is exposed and to which anyone can fall victim. Man's susceptibility to loneliness is built into him; it is part of his biological inheritance. And this constitutional susceptibility is reinforced by a multitude of social and cultural factors.

Loneliness is not the disease of being alone; being alone is in the deepest sense the human condition. It is the disease of feeling alone, of feeling isolated, cut off from human contact and human warmth. Some people battle all their lives against this poignant emotion, struggling constantly to come to terms with the immutable fact of their existence: the fact that all human beings are separate, one from another, and will remain so all their lives; each sealed within the thin envelope of skin in which he is contained. If this struggle is successful, the individual ultimately transcends that physical limitation and becomes most himself precisely because he is closely bound to others.

Those who are lonely erect all kinds of defenses against the disease. They may hide it behind all sorts of symptoms and behavior. They may experience it as depression, or as anger, or as panic, or as a vague, uneasy feeling that something, somewhere, is not quite as it should be. Whatever the disguise it wears, however the individual attempts to protect himself from it, loneliness is both frightening and painful.

But the battle against loneliness can be won. The disease can be treated and eventually cured. This cure does not lie in trying to evade it or in throwing up defenses against it or in ignoring it. Nor can loneliness be assuaged by the mere physical presence of other people; we often feel most desolate and most alone in the midst of crowds. The cure for loneliness lies in facing it and understanding it. Some people achieve such understanding almost unconsciously, in the very process of living and growing, and so are at least partially immunized against the disease. But no one can avoid it all his life. The healthy person must learn to recognize it when it appears, to cope with its pangs when they assail him, and to meet its appearance without terror or panic. And those who cannot be their own physicians can find help through the methods of modern psychotherapy.

In this process the patient looks back into his past and into the misty memories of the early experiences that shaped his attitudes and his growth. When finally he raises his ghosts from the deep caverns of the unconscious in which they have made their homes, when he exposes them to the clear light of conscious understanding, they vanish. When he learns the causes of his disease, he can treat it.

The causes of any disease, whether of the body or of the emotions, are usually complex—a whole network of interrelated factors—and the disease of loneliness is no exception. Each human being carries within himself constitutional qualities that predispose him to loneliness, and if these are not balanced by the social factor of a healthy environment—both in the home and in the broader cultural milieu—it is more than likely that he will fall victim to the disease.

Every story of loneliness is a tragedy. It is a tale of wasted effort and wasted love in which there are many villains: all the deep unconscious forces that keep the lonely man or woman from facing and conquering his problem. The stories that follow are simplified; they present the broad, general outlines of each situation rather than the specific details; they by-pass many of the villains who must be defeated if the conquest of loneliness is finally to be achieved. Nevertheless, although the stories are, in a sense, schematic, each will serve to point at one of the biological factors that must be understood if loneliness, no matter from whence it springs, is to be undone.

The fourteen-year-old was quite a pretty girl. That is, she would have been pretty had she not looked so tense, so frightened; had she not tightened her lips and rubbed her hands nervously across her face.

"Why have you come to see me?" I asked her.

"The teacher said I should. . . . Maybe it's because of what happened yesterday."

"Would you care to tell me about it?"

"The whole class went out into the woods for a picnic. To a place where I go a lot by myself, after school." Her taut face became soft and wistful. "It's so quiet. Sometimes I hear little twigs crackling under my feet. But otherwise there's no sound. . . . And it's pretty—the trees and the haze between the trunks. . . ."

I nodded.

"I used to like being there by myself. In the city, I feel suffocated by the houses and the streets and all the people. I feel that way in school, too, and at home. But in the woods I feel better. No one else around. Not my mother to bawl me out or the boys to tease me. Just me and—nothing . . ."

She sighed, and then the drawn look came back to her face.

"Well, yesterday, when we were all out there together, I went off. I walked for a while. It was very still . . . Then all of a sudden I got this horrible feeling. My throat got all tight and it seemed as if I was choking. My legs and arms and hands seemed to become gigantic and strange. I looked at them . . . I didn't know whose they were. It was as if they didn't belong to me any more—as if I didn't belong to myself. As if I was a complete stranger. It was . . . just horrible." She moved her hands tentatively and helplessly.

"And then what did you do?"

"I began to run—to get away from that feeling—from . . . from . . ." Her voice trailed off.

"Did the feeling disappear?"

"Yes, when I reached the others. I was all out of breath. My lungs felt as if they would burst. But I felt better. Quieter. Like myself again."

What was this "horrible feeling" that appeared so suddenly, so dramatically, so frighteningly? What was wrong with this girl? She was neither stupid nor foolish; she was bright and sensible, and although she had always been something of a daydreamer, rather quiet and withdrawn, she was a good student. But she was lonely—and she had suddenly become conscious of her loneliness by becoming conscious of herself: of her muscles, of her breath, of the heart beating within her, the eyes in her head, the thinking inside that head. There she stood, inside herself, feeling her own strangeness. It was as if she were someone else, as if she had jumped away from herself, staring at the creature that was she.

The experience of depersonalization, of suddenly losing one's sense of self, is an overwhelming one. It is loneliness carried to the point of panic. For the girl this was, fortunately, the first and only attack; in treatment she found the roots of the loneliness that had erupted in such a terrorizing fashion. But if the attack had recurred, if the warning had not been heeded in time, the child might have become seriously ill.

The capacity to feel this sense of depersonalization seems to be specifically and uniquely human, part of man's biological inheritance. To lose one's sense of identity, one must first have it. And one respect in which man is distinguished from all the life that mills around him in endless activity is that he possesses self-awareness.

Flowers live and breathe, just as do people. There is an exchange of oxygen between them and their surroundings, there is a continuing process of growth and development. Tomorrow there may be a tiny bud where today there is only a bare stalk, and in a few days there will be a fine scent and a delicate little blossom. But although the flower breathes and lives and grows, just as we do, it does not know, as far as science has been able to discover, that it does.

A dog will answer to his name. If his master calls him, he will scamper over, wagging his tail. He will look at his owner with tender brown eyes and nuzzle him with a moist nose. He will bark, he will all but speak. But he is not conscious of himself and of what he is doing; he is conscious of the human being he loves. He is more aware than is the plant, but he will never achieve the self-consciousness that makes human beings human.

An old Brahman legend has it that once, thousands of years ago, a man threw a stone over his head and cried out, "OM—I am." That was the birth of man.

The Bible story of the Garden of Eden, although different in its particulars, says very much the same thing. For this is the story not only of how God created man, but of how man became human. The drama of Eve's temptation by the serpent too often obscures the real core and meaning of the tale.

In the Garden of Eden, where Adam and Eve dwelt, were two special trees, among the many others. One was the tree of knowledge; the other, mentioned casually, almost in passing, the tree of life. The fruit of this tree was not forbidden; of it Adam and Eve could eat. And had they been content to abide by God's command, they would still be there, in the Garden of Eden, living the life of dreamy, instinctual delectation that is given to all creatures but man. But because Adam and Eve ate of the forbidden fruit, they were expelled from Eden. By their trespass they became human; they knew that they were naked. Wisely God had warned them against eating the poisonous fruit of self-awareness. And now never again could man return to those early days of blissful delight. His self-consciousness, his cognition, changed the content and the very rhythm of his existence.

Before they ate of the forbidden fruit, Adam and Eve lived in a twilight world of utter protection and warmth. They did not have either to work or to strive. Such a world every man once knew. For nine idyllic months the human embryo lolls in its mother's womb, comfortable, secure, at peace. But then, like Adam and Eve, it is expelled from its paradise. From the warm fluidity of the womb, from that chamber of safety and security, it is abruptly banished, exiled into a strange and frightening world. The light hurts the infant's eyes, the noise hurts its ears, the touch of solid objects hurts its skin. The air sears its lungs, new to the strange sensation of breathing. And as his introduction into all these terrors, the new-born has to negotiate the suffocating, viselike straits of his mother's birth canal.

Unlike Adam and Eve on their explusion, however, the infant is not yet self-aware. He is alone, but not yet lonely. He gropes and flails toward his mother for protection and sustenance, and although this groping is the first gesture toward the outside help he will need forever after, the infant does not yet realize that the help he needs comes from somewhere beyond himself. In the first few months of his life, he does not experience his mother as a separate being. Though flung from her womb, he still lives partially within her. For he does not draw a line between himself and the rest of the universe. Slowly, during the first year of his existence, he learns to make this differentiation. His ego is formed—his sense of self comes into being. From now on, he is self-conscious, and so he is susceptible to loneliness.

The child will have no protection against the disease if his mother, his first and closest link to the world, is self-involved, anxious, preoccupied with her own loneliness, hostile, rejecting. He will assimilate these traits into his psychic character just as surely and insidiously as if they had come down to him in his very genes. The built-in threat of loneliness contained in his human self-awareness can thus be enormously magnified.

Man's self-awareness, then, predisposes him to loneliness. It is, however, not the only cause. There are others, equally important, and it would be a serious mistake to assume, in any given case, that only one factor was at work.

Thus, the young girl's moment of panic was the result not only of her haunting encounter with herself, but also of the rising adolescent tide of sexuality. Gradually, in subsequent conversations, the girl learned how her newly awakened desires, which her rigid and rejecting home environment had left her unprepared to meet, had contributed to her loneliness and to her panic. She was frightened of boys, unconsciously afraid they would injure her. The only release she could find for her sexual drive was in the gratifying yet deeply disturbing act of masturbation.

The sex drive, both in its biological and its psychological aspects, is another of man's built-in endowments which, improperly understood and improperly used, can lead to loneliness and deep anguish.

The ancients seem to have known this, too. The old Greek myth tells us of the handsome youth, Narcissus, who became enamored of his own image, reflected in the still waters of a river. Stretching out his arms toward his beloved, to clasp him to himself, he slipped into the deep waters and drowned.

This legend contains a profound pyschological truth. The sexual urge and the drive toward love, with which the legend of Narcissus concerns itself, have, of course, a biological base and a biological function. Beyond that, however, this instinctual drive, which psychoanalysis calls libido, is directed toward the preservation of the race, and is part of the whole psychic make-up of man. It is rooted in sex, but transcends it. Turned outwards, toward the world, it underlies all our social development and all our cultural achievements. It is the cement that holds men together. To consider man's sex drive merely as a biological function and its expression merely as an animal activity, to neglect its key position as the cornerstone of human culture, is to rob man of his humanity.

For when the libidinal drive finds a normal outlet, as under normal circumstances it does, it links two individu-

als, man and woman, in a relationship of closeness and
mutuality. In this way it constructs a bridge between the
individual and the outside world, between his biological
and social inheritances. By integrating the individual into
his world, it provides the strongest defense against loneliness. But if, through a failure or a distortion of development, the libidinal drive is turned inwards, toward the self,
emotional illness is bound to occur.

Those who take a purely biological approach to sex, and
treat it as if it had no significant psychological elements,
almost inevitably encourage such a result. Nevertheless,
because sex is partly a biological phenomenon, we must
understand something of its effect on the body if we are to
understand its effect on the emotions and on the mind.

The bodies of both men and women contain sex glands
—ovaries in the female, testicles in the male. Each of these
organs bears in its excretion cell units (ova and semen)
which, combined, produce the material necessary to create a
new individual. In addition, these glands produce hormones which, streaming into the blood, induce a certain
tension we call the sex drive. This tension, like any other,
cries for deliverance. It can be released either by mechanical
local self-stimulation (masturbation), or by the link of the
male and female sex organs. Only this second choice can
span across the abyss of isolation to the reality of another
individual. For masturbation, although it serves to release
the stored-up physical tensions, leaves the individual in his
self-gratifying loneliness and isolation. These are basic
organic factors that reach decisively into the total character
and the emotional superstructure of man's psychic life.

Still another story may bring this into sharper focus. It
concerns a ship's doctor on one of the great transatlantic
lines who came for psychiatric help because he was

frightened of his own aggressive impulses, frightened that one day they would overwhelm him and he would do something violently destructive.

His mother had died when he was three years old. He had never known his father, a drunken derelict who had deserted the mother even before their baby was born. The child was brought up by his grandfather, a sullen old widower who grudgingly did his duty by the child—but no more. He had no use for the unwanted intruder.

Through his own efforts, and with no outside help, the young man completed medical school. Then, instead of opening his own practice or continuing to work on the staff of the hospital in which he had taken his postgraduate training, he took a position which, by its very nature, insulated him from any close human contact. The passengers came and went. A gulf of status separated the doctor from most of the crew.

And yet this lonely occupation had a real attraction for him. The huge bulk of the ship somehow symbolized his long-dead mother's womb, in which he could feel the safety and security he had never previously known.

He had never had any love relationship with a woman; he knew only casual affairs and the impersonal business transactions of prostitution. Once he began to work on the ship, his only sexual outlet was in masturbation.

Most of the time, he liked his job. During the day he was kept busy attending to an endless procession of minor complaints, both from the passengers and from the crew, and so he had no time to worry. But at night, he would stand on the forward deck for hours, leaning over the railing and staring into the dark waters that flowed beneath the ship in never-ending phosphorescent waves. He would look up at the moon and down into its silvery reflection in the sea. Flickering stars and planets hung suspended in the sky.

He would stand musing for a while and then, from the darkness surrounding him, he would hear the deep voice of the sailor on watch, singing a melancholy chanty. This, somehow, was always more than the doctor could bear and, overcome by a feeling of terrorized abandonment, he would turn and walk with uncertain steps toward midship. There, through the transparent curtains of the saloon bar, he could make out the warm, golden glow of the intimate room. He would look in, like a child with his nose pressed against a bakery window, and watch the elegantly dressed passengers sipping their drinks, talking, laughing, dancing to the tunes of an orchestra he could neither see nor hear. Inside was champagne, gaiety, warmth. Outside was only loneliness and anger. Suddenly the doctor would feel an almost uncontrollable impulse to smash the glass that separated him from the others, to leap into the room, to sweep all the glasses off the bar, to fill the air with the tinkling and crashing of crystal—to destroy, to annihilate everything in his path. Once, he almost did, but the impulse lasted only for a moment. Why couldn't he go through with it? Why couldn't he?

That his aggression was related to his profound loneliness, and that his loneliness was related to his inability to make any meaningful sexual contact, seemed obvious. His early life had not taught him the primary lesson of how to reach across the chasm that separates one human being from another. Always a glass window stood between him and his fellow men; not knowing how to open it, and wanting to, desperately, he felt impelled to smash it. He had never had the experience of a close relationship of any kind and he had turned his sex drive—his drive toward others—back on himself. And so he had become more and more encapsulated in his own loneliness.

One more factor should be added to this biological constellation: the inescapable fact of death. A profound terror of this unfathomable nothingness, this cessation of life, of warmth, of movement, is one of the threatening ghosts that lurks deep in the canyons of everyone's mind. Under normal circumstances, however, this fear is not consciously perceived. If it were man's constant companion, if it walked and talked with him twenty-four hours a day, life would be unbearable. But from time to time, when the individual is exposed to a situation of actual or imagined danger, or when someone dies who has been close to him, this choking fear creeps up, leaving him with a feeling of utter desolation and loss.

Once I listened to the story of a childhood experience that had left a deeper imprint on the development of a man's character than had any of the subsequent events of his life.

This life had not been uneventful. Born into wealth and position, the man had lived to see the whole structure of his existence crumble under the impact of the Hitler persecution. He had been compelled to leave his country, his home, his money—all in one anguished hour. He had stood up under this blow and all the additional strains that were added to it: when he left his homeland, his wife was pregnant, he was penniless and without roots. And he was in actual danger of his life.

He had fought his way through to a new existence more glamorous and in many respects more satisfactory than the one he had been forced to leave.

Then finally the breakdown came. Paradoxically enough, the very childhood experience which had so fortified him that he could withstand the trials history had imposed was at least partially responsible for his current illness. When I saw him, he was suffering from a stomach ulcer, the bodily expression of his shattered emotions.

What was this experience? It had been a meeting with death in a frame of extraordinary beauty. When he was about twelve years old, the boy had been asked to keep the honor watch for his dead uncle throughout the first night. The older man had considerable money, and, in his later years, after resigning as president of his gigantic business enterprise, had become intensely interested in flowers. Indeed, they had become his ruling passion, and in the middle of the city he had built a fantastic island, a house of glass, containing thousands upon thousands of flowers. The only room that was not given over to them was his study, through whose sliding glass doors he could look out at the dazzling glory of the indoor garden he had thus constructed.

When he died, his corpse reposed in state in this very study. During the long night of watching, while a merciless rain kept drumming on the glass roof, the child stared at the noble, motionless, pale face he had known so well. Every corner of the room was filled with flowers; people from all over the country had sent the tribute they knew the unusual man would have most appreciated. Their tropical scent and heavy perfume numbed the boy's senses. Confronted, for the first time, through all the endless, frightening hours of the night, with the incomprehensible enigma of death, he felt the triumphant glory of his own life with a bittersweet taste he never lost.

At the funeral, when the casket was at last lowered, he,

like everyone else, took a clod of earth from the shovel and threw it into the grave. It made a dull sound as it struck the box, and he thought: "Where is he now? Where am I? And who am I, myself?"

This unusual encounter with death had tremendous impact on the child. It had a protective quality; the setting had been of such exquisite beauty that it robbed the experience of at least part of its sting. But it had a traumatic character, too; it was more than he could assimilate. And so it became the fertile soil in which the harrowing experiences of his later life took root and grew far beyond the safety mark. Now he could no longer tolerate his feelings of desertion and loss. The experience was the largest single contributing factor in his illness, although certainly not the only one.

The deep-seated biological characteristics discussed in this chapter are threats to every man. The unconscious awareness of time, of each minute that brings him closer to the uncertain adventure of death, the anxiety associated with his self-awareness and finally his libidinal drives—with these everyone must cope. In addition to this biological heritage, each man has to live on a social level, in a mechanized, materialistic, impersonal civilization, for which he is not prepared at birth and to which he may never adjust. Here is another, even more fateful ground for his loneliness.

CHAPTER TWO

❖

Of Must and Misery

MAN MOVES ON two levels simultaneously, the biological
and the sociological. They are closely interrelated; biology
itself, in its drive to preserve the race, points instinctively
from one individual to the other, from man to woman and
from woman to man. This simple and basic truth explains
not only the need for mutual adjustment between individuals, but in its extension lies behind the whole development of society and of the individual as a social being.
The social need that derives from man's biological inheritance should be, then, one of the main tools with which to
overcome loneliness.

However, the tragic fact is that from the prehistoric days
of the original clan, when society first began to evolve,
both the necessary rules, laws and limitations and man's
ingenious technical and mechanical inventions have so
frustrated humanity that they have almost wrecked the
original design, and have tended to exaggerate loneliness
rather than to dissolve it. Somehow the shimmering curve
of social evolution has been bent against itself, and the
individual, in a fateful spiral and at an ever increasing
tempo, has fallen deeper and deeper into isolation. Something has gone wrong with the great master plan, and the
paradoxical truth is that at the very moment when
technological development and social organization have

increased to the maximum man's chances for the communication that bridges the chasm between individuals, humanity seems to suffer from a greater loneliness than ever before, from a loneliness that lays its dark hands with suffocating pressure over the tormented earth.

Man seems, in his social and technological development, to have lost his way, to have deviated so far from his original biological heritage that he is now completely and hopelessly bewildered by himself and his world.

The very existence of technology and social organization bears witness to the extraordinary development of human intelligence. But man's cortex, the creative part of his brain, has jumped ahead of his emotions. They lag far behind, unable to catch up and to reconcile him to his relatively recent evolutionary acquisition: inventive genius. The functioning of the human mind has become so complicated that nearly all the man-made machines work more efficiently than the very brains that devised them. This dichotomy between intellect and emotions becomes glaringly evident in man's hectic battle against a daily routine that in too many cases leaves him dissatisfied, miserable and lonely.

What does the world we have created actually look like? What about our vaunted technical achievements?

It is a truism to state that this is the machine age. Push a button and a bell rings; an electric organ plays Bach cantatas; a gas flame spends its blue heat to boil the water for someone's breakfast egg; car motors begin to hum; the air becomes "conditioned"; and a thousand lights burn in a thousand glass bulbs.

This technical climate in itself need be no problem; it could be easily mastered if it were recognized as the frame and not taken for the picture. As it happens, however, the human being is born uncritical; the infant finds his world ready-made and he takes it all in. He does not discriminate. He does not realize the difference between a flower (life) and the lens (technology) through which he can look at its magnified petals, between an ox and the tin can in which its meat is packed. He cannot distinguish the difference in principle between the mechanics of an icebox and the structure of a cloud. He does not realize that the leather of his shoes was once the skin of a calf, cavorting in some distant pasture, that the wood of the chair on which he sits came from an old shade tree, that the wool of his jacket was once a sheep's coat, that the silk of his clothes was made by a little worm somewhere in endless China, and that the feathers of his pillow were the clothing of cackling white geese.

The child begins his life confused, and his confusion grows with him. Reality moves ever further and further away until he can recognize neither his own nature nor the nature of the world. The earth's once noble features have become ugly, distorted and falsified, and the world man himself has created stares at him with glittering, dead eyes; the sparkling, fascinating brilliance of its façade cannot hide the empty shadows behind it. What is even worse, modern man seems to be afraid to keep even the residues of nature close to him. All over the earth the dead matter expands triumphantly; the man-made miracles—and the mechanized death of steel, glass, fiber, artificial dye, and artificial nylon —threaten to engulf the world. Less and less can man identify with his surroundings, less and less can he find his own image, or something akin to it, reflected in these dead waters of technical contrivances.

Every day the newspapers report on the new wonders

developed by the modern alchemists—industrial scientists, electronics engineers and physicists. Every day brings its promise of new gadgets and new "advances." As if the tempo of modern life was not fast enough, we hear that the day is not far away when jet planes will circle the earth in minutes. As if the radio, the telephone and television had not already sufficiently invaded privacy, we are assured a future in which the malignant electronic eye can follow us everywhere. As if mother earth had not already been scarred and mutilated, new miracles of construction are proposed, which may disfigure her face beyond all recognition.

Death closes in from all sides. The stars disappear behind the screaming neon lights and the stony, straight façades of the skyscrapers in the rectangular streets. The obtrusive, monotonous clatter of the typewriters, the drumming noises of the motors in powerhouses and airplanes and the searing stench of gasoline exhaust—these have become the symbols of a time of unparalleled technical achievement, which has so outstripped man's emotions and which has brought him so far from his own nature that the poor psyche can only cringe and coil back into a bewildered and devastated loneliness.

Sometimes the naïve sentences of a simple soul bring a rare and sudden clarity to a clouded vista. "Coming home one night in the subway, I saw the stars for three stations," a depressed young girl said. "Then the elevated train raced down again under the earth, and there were only the electric bulbs on the drab ceiling, the stuffy air, and the smelly people around me. The stars for three stations—that's all." The remark may have been sentimental, full of a dubious romanticism, but it was, nevertheless, the expression of a truth.

Granted that technology has increased the power of the individual a million times, how does that help him? Once he had nothing but the strength of his own body, his arms and hands and legs. The stronger arms smashed the weaker ones and the quicker legs eluded the slower ones. The law of nature was the law of human life. It was, in many respects, a cruel law, but it was simple. It could be understood. And, more important, it corresponded to man's own basic structure.

Everything has changed since then, both man's values and the means by which he acquires them. The power of arms and legs has been increased by thousands of devices: one finger can trigger off a machine gun or hold the stick of an H-bomb-carrying airplane, one toe can push the ignition of an automobile. The radius of man's experience has been immeasurably lengthened; words and ideas and feelings of peoples and nations in all corners of the earth have become part of each man's daily life. Humanity has won an amazing victory over time and space. Our grandfathers and even our fathers were more or less glued to the places in which they lived. They had no refrigerators, no telephones, no electric lights. Their lives were small and limited in comparison with ours. But were they, as people, less fulfilled, less happy? Has technology helped man's emotional development? Or has it not rather chased him into a deeper isolation, into a more malignant type of loneliness?

Nobody chose the specific culture into which he was born, or the place, the language or the time he lives in. Everyone is pushed into the world without being asked, and everyone is from birth overwhelmed and confused by the degree to which Homo sapiens has changed both his own original biological inheritance and the world of nature

around him. Technology has certainly created more comfort for the body, has improved hygiene and increased the
quantity of man's experiences. Nor are its advances at an
end. But none of them will really touch him, if they are
not geared to his basic nature. They leave the center of
his emotions dry. They give him nothing but a cold, intellectual appreciation.

This process of alienation, by which man moves further
and further from the basic ground on which his life is
founded, reminds one of Perseus's struggle with the giant
whose strength returned whenever he touched the earth.
It was not until Perseus finally succeeded in lifting him
high off the ground and holding him in the air, that he
was able to kill him. Nowadays people leave the big cities
to "re-create" themselves, go to the country to "get away
from it all." Away from what? Why live in a situation one
has to get away from? Is it only technology and its obtrusive
noise that makes everyone run?

Our cultural organization is no less deforming; it has
established norms of behavior just as artificial as the "genuine leather simulated plastic overnight bag" sold in the
shiny glass and chromium drugstore on the corner. The
human race has hidden its own nature from itself not only
by the man-made constructions of technology, but by the
man-made constructions of social values and social rules as
well. And the ones by which the Western world guides
itself exaggerate inner conflict and thus increase the tendency to withdrawal and retreat.

The greatest, most disastrous confusion with which man
has yoked himself began with the invention of money. And
the yoke has become more choking as the craving for money
has become more obsessive and compulsive. In our culture
the point has been reached at which men are judged less

for their abilities than for their bank accounts, and these bank accounts by no means need reflect the value of the man or of his accomplishments. On the contrary, it is characteristic of our society that the so-called intellectual professions, the professions with the highest social value—teaching, science and journalism, for example—are among the lowest paid.

What is even worse, money seems to fatten on itself. He who has more, gets more; it is difficult to become rich and easy to become richer. How can the individual trust a world that operates on such a basis, how can he find any sense in so intrinsically a senseless pattern? When the endless chase after money, the pointless, self-defeating struggle to make more and to get more, is piled on top of all the other pressures to which man is subjected by his own nature, by his technology and by the other aspects of his culture, it is not surprising that the individual should so often retreat into disease and despair. I have heard, over and over, in countless variations, stories of money and tragedy, money and illness, money and loneliness. I have listened, each time with the same shocked amazement, to innumerable tales of the hectic and sick race for money, the frantic pursuit of an ever sinking horizon, a race that keeps all the runners chasing through the long and empty hallways of their loneliness until they collapse—never having achieved what they wanted. This murderous marathon is utterly exhausting; the number of heart collapses as the result of "business worries" is an index of the degree to which man has moved away from his original nature and his original soil.

One of these stories concerns an extremely prosperous businessman. I have known him for many years; he has always been wealthy and every year he becomes wealthier. Each time we meet he complains that he does not enjoy his work, that he hates the fiercely competitive grind that keeps him going until late at night, scheming and planning for ways to increase his already more than substantial income. He has suffered from various diseases of psychogenic origin for a long time; he knows that if he keeps going at his present pace he is bound to collapse. And for as long as I have known him, he has assured me that he does not intend to keep on working, that his ambition is to retire and to live simply on a moderate income as soon as he has enough money to take care of his minimum wants. He already has more than enough. He knows it. Yet he has not stopped working. And he will not, until he drops in his traces, the victim of his own senseless striving for more and more, trapped in the vicious circle he has drawn around himself.

The dangerous, destructive impact of money is most dramatically illustrated by the story of a young Hungarian couple, whose lives were wrecked almost beyond repair when money was suddenly heaped lavishly upon them.

Sascha was a violinist. He was talented and successful and held promise of even greater achievement. Music was nearly all his life; though not quite all. He was passionately devoted to his attractive young wife, Tessa, and to their infant son.

The child had a fine, pale face. Blue veins were visible under the transparent skin of his tiny hands, and his whole chiseled body was fragile—of an almost glassy consistency. His delicacy only heightened his parents' tenderness. The mother would sit by his cradle for hours, crooning to him. The father often interrupted his practicing to walk into the child's room, hoping, by playing one of the gypsy tunes whose fiery rhythms made the baby jump in frightened joy, to bring a tiny smile to the lucid face.

The days and years passed in joyous harmony. The child developed into a shy and lanky youngster, Sascha's increasing artistic maturity led him from one success to the next, and the marriage grew in depth and meaning.

One day word came that Tessa's father had died. He had been one of the great Hungarian landowners, a brittle, taciturn and lonely man who, after the early death of his wife, had shut himself up in seclusion and showed little or no interest in his daughter. When the report of his death reached her, Tessa was relatively untouched. For a moment she felt a sharp stab of self-pity and a rush of bitterness against this father who had never given her any attention. When she and Sascha married, she had asked him to support his son-in-law's study and to finance his first conceit appearance. The father had refused, brusquely, just as he had refused, all through her childhood, to give her the love she needed and wanted. Now it all came back to her in a flood of painful recollection, and for a while she toyed with the idea of not taking the money she had inherited; the idea of making the ultimate gesture of defiance, of paying her father back in death for what he had not done for her during his lifetime.

Sascha, however, was not impressed by such heroics. His family had been poor; his father and mother had struggled all their lives. He remembered the deprivations and the constant pressures of his childhood. His mother had nagged at him continually to practice, so that he could become rich and famous and could repay her for all the "sacrifices" she had made for "his" sake. Now he had achieved success. He had done it entirely on his own. He was entitled to all the good things life could offer him. The money would not make him give up his music; nothing could do that. It would only add to the joy he and Tessa knew in one another, their baby, their work and their friends.

Tessa yielded. Soon the couple were deep in a conversation about the inheritance: how big was it going to be; which lawyer should they hire to represent them; should they buy a house in the country or remain in the city; should they tour the European capitals or take a trip around the world; should they invest in stocks, bonds, real estate, jewelry or art?

For the first few weeks, they were so busy putting their affairs in order that Sascha could not find the time to practice. Tessa urged him to take up his violin, but he felt nervous and jumpy. He resented her nagging. She was like his mother, always after him to practice when he wanted to play. He decided to put his violin to rest for a short time. He never took it up again.

The couple moved into a sumptuously furnished house and staffed it with maids, butlers and footmen. Gradually— almost imperceptibly at first—their friends and their personalities changed. Before, they had been surrounded by musicians, painters, writers, actors. Now their home was a meeting place for bankers, politicians, lawyers, heads of giant corporations. Instead of the inspired singing of the violin, the silent and devoted study of books, the warm conversation of friends and the tender chatter of the two lovers, there was now the false and forced cordiality of business transactions behind the blue smoke of expensive cigars. There were drinks and poker games and aimless conversations.

When each night the door finally shut behind the last guest and the two were alone together, husband and wife could find nothing to say to one another. Their relationship seemed to have evaporated in the aroma of the exquisite food, the delicate wines, the heavy cigars and the hectic excitement of new plans for new money. A gray, sinking silence settled down on them; each was overcome by a feeling of embarrassed emptiness and solitude. Each looked for some sort of escape from the unbearable, meaningless monotony and loneliness of their life together.

Sascha soon found a mistress, on whom he lavished all his attentions. Tessa at first plunged into a whirl of social and charitable activities and then, without any warning, retreated into sullen melancholy. The separation came, as it had to, and after this the couple met only twice: the first time during the divorce proceedings, and the second time . . .

The child had been of a sickly constitution from the beginning. I have never been able to determine the exact nature of his original ailment—I do not know whether it had to do with the ductless glands, or with a leukemic condition of the blood, or with a tubercular infection. Whatever caused the initial constitutional weakness, however, it seems almost certain that the sudden worsening of the child's condition, which began almost simultaneously with his parents' divorce, was not accidental. That there is an intimate relationship between our emotional life and the functioning of our body cells is an established fact; innumerable studies and experiments have borne it out. A human being is an entity; any disturbance, whether it takes place in the body or in the emotions, produces symptoms that alter the entire functioning of the organism. This child simply wilted away. His body revolted against the unbearable disruption of his life, of the bonds that had tied his beloved parents to one another and to him. He died.

And so, after half a year of separation, the parents met.

again at their child's funeral. They did not speak to one
another. They did not look at one another. Each listened
silently to the organ music. Each stared silently at the
small white face in the casket. When the services were over,
each got into his waiting car, wrapped in a mute daze of
spite and sick despair.

When I saw the wife shortly thereafter, she stared at me
with an empty face. Her hands were covered with huge
diamonds, and her once beautiful features seemed old and
broken.

"If only I could cry," she whispered. "If you could only
make me cry . . ."

I have told this story in rather complete detail because I
feel that its tragic elements highlight a dangerous cultural
trend of which the overvaluation of money is only one
aspect. For in our culture, the individual, with all his
newly acquired power, with all his material conveniences,
with all his technical achievements, has been pushed into
the position of a slave, so that he is no longer free to live
in accordance with his own inner character and needs.

High on the list of cultural oppressions stands the
problem of making a living. A man's profession too often
traps him in a tight ring from which there seems to be no
escape. I still remember vividly the sulky and superior
expression on the face of the eighteen-year-old lad whose
father had brought him for "vocational guidance." This
father was a driving, successful businessman who had always
taken it for granted that his son would join the family
business and, if possible, expand the already huge corporation. But this the son obstinately refused to do. The father,
who had, after all, to live up to his image of himself as a

"tolerant, modern, democratic parent," was willing to make a compromise.

"If he won't go into the business, he's got to study and become something. After all, he can't just sit around and write poetry. A man must have a profession."

"Why must he?" the son answered dryly. His behavior and his apparently aimless mode of life were the overt expression of his deep resentment against his father, against the overbearing self-importance, intolerant smugness and narrow-minded arrogance the lad sensed under the "liberal" façade. Well, why must he? Why must such a boy—or indeed any boy—have a profession or a skill? Why must he become a doctor or a lawyer, an architect or a physicist, a grocer or a mechanic? Why must he direct his life into one specific channel and limit it to one small segment of activity? Why not have all of it, the whole show?

Because life simply cannot function that way. Because everyone lives in a social group. And every social group has its rules and standards, all of which cut deeply into the freedom of the individual, asking for sacrifices, and demanding that each serve the good of the whole through the narrow contribution he can make in his chosen field.

Intellectually, this limitation of activity is expected and accepted with such ease that it seems almost trite to state it. But the fact is that emotionally everyone resists it, and only comes to terms with it after considerable anguish, the anguish of growing up. For as he matures and becomes an adult, capable of making his own way in the world, the individual discovers that the childhood situation is being repeated. He no longer has to meet his parents' rules and regulations and demands, he has cast off one yoke. But now he is strapped into another: the rules, regulations and demands of society. If he does not submit to them, he is pushed into the role of the ostracized, the outcast or the ridiculous dreamer; he is pushed into loneliness.

The eighteen-year-old lad will probably have to give up his resistance against his father in some not-too-distant future. When he matures he will have to recognize that he cannot devote his entire life to his rebellion, that he cannot make the whole fabric of society the surrogate for his father, that he must come to terms with the realities of life and the restrictions of society. He will have to compromise. If he does not, if he sticks to the isolation of his chosen idleness, he will probably be headed for severe trouble, for the self-created loneliness of dilettante bohemianism, neurosis or psychosis, unless he is that one in a million who, as an artist, succeeds, by listening to the lonely voices within himself, in molding the world after his own image. (That unusual personality structure will be examined later in this book, in a special chapter on the meaning of art.)

Everyone who is frozen into the modern mechanized mold rebels against it, although his rebellion may not even be conscious. He feels isolated, powerless and trapped, and usually accepts his fate with an expression of tired resentment, depression and hostility. Only in rare instances, in a very strong and powerful character, does the inner revolt erupt into reality, does the individual refuse to hew to a line he himself always basically rejected.

Marc worked for a vast construction company. He shared an office with another man in one of the new steel and glass buildings that have all the advantages of hygiene and all the boredom of nothing but hygiene. Eight hours a day, five days a week, Marc sat glued to his desk, bent over calculations, digits and figures. He was only one little cog in the great wheel that spun out the electrification of countries and continents, the construction of enormous reservoirs and canals, and the production of gadgets and devices on whose functioning hundreds of thousands of lives depended. His was only a tiny section of all that industrial glory, and often it occurred to him that he did not even know the spot on the great master plan into which his particular calculations would be fitted. Although Marc was aware that his work was important, and that his most trivial error could cost someone his life, he felt that his ingenuity and his training were being wasted. The mechanical, monotonous, repetitious job was grinding him down, and he felt an increasing weariness and depression. Weekends, spent in the company of his well-meaning, but uninspiring wife, failed to compensate for the daily tedium; he became irascible, bad-tempered and quarrelsome, and the smallest incidents annoyed him out of all proportion.

One day, a nearly completed building collapsed, taking the life of one laborer and severely injuring several others, who were dug out of the debris only after hours of frantic work. Marc's corporation had designed the building, and the investigation that followed the tragic accident hinted at the likelihood that something had been wrong with the original plans. Although the court took no action, the disaster had a castastrophic effect on Marc. He had not been a member of the team responsible for this particular project, yet he continued to identify with it. He fell into an increasingly severe depression, seriously contemplated suicide and regained his perspective only after psychoanalytic treatment led him to understand that unconsciously he had been hoping for this disaster, that time and time again he had been tempted to write down the wrong specifications on his blueprints, that he had been toying with the idea of producing the very calamity that had occurred.

These destructive fantasies had been an expression of his utter desperation and of his bitter resentment at being forced to follow a daily routine that made no sense to him at all. As it turned out, only the day before the accident he had remarked to the man with whom he shared his office that such a thing might happen, and he was sure this "premonition" had made his colleague suspect that Marc had intentionally caused the disaster.

Civilization shows itself in another frightening social development: the office. Something buried deep in everyone's mind is sickened by this modern instrument of slavery and torture. The fixed hours, the fixed and limited activities and the fixed frame of functioning are, no less than the impersonal assembly line, strait jackets on human creativity. For three quarters of his waking day, the average office worker gives up his right to think, decide and act for himself. Secretaries pound away monotonously at their typewriters for the sake of selling or buying soap, linen, battleships, books, jewels and airplanes. Bookkeepers total up long columns of meaningless figures, clerks file away papers in which they have no interest. And behind every worker is the boss—friendly or unfriendly, aloof or back-slapping—driving his employees because he in turn is being driven: by the need to make more money, by the worries of competition, by the demands of his wife and his children who, for the sake of his prestige, must have fur coats and "good" educations. Nobody lives as he would like to, and the result of all this frustration is restless hate and a masochistic retreat into splendid isolation.

Culture imposes still other rules and demands: his economic position forces the "good citizen" to live in certain sections of the city or in certain suburbs; social obligations compel him to see people and call them friends when in fact he may despise them.

This artificial thicket of social and economic obligations is summed up in the cocktail party, that personification of loneliness. The cocktail party is not really a social event, nor is it a means of exchanging ideas or enjoying old or new friendships. At base it is a commercial institution, at which one transacts business or makes contact with those "important" people who may in the future be useful in providing new steps on the long and rickety ladder to social and financial success. The host and hostess shamelessly invite people in whom they have not the slightest interest, in the hope that they will in turn be invited to their guests' homes to meet *their* friends, whom they will then invite to their homes, and so on and on in the same calculated circle.

This hectic game is repeated, of course in less blatant fashion and to a lesser degree, in all the organizations to which the "good citizen" belongs. Our American passion for joining—sororities, fraternities, civic organizations, booster clubs, professional societies, political clubs, church auxiliaries—is in large measure both a reflection and a proof of an increasing sense of isolation. Many men and women seek refuge from loneliness in the enforced and sanctimonious cordiality of group activity, sailing under the proud flag of true democracy. Everybody lives everybody else's life, and the "good citizen" is involved in onion-like layers of participation and obligation. Starting with his interest in his own neighbors and neighborhood, his frontiers of activity always expand—not only morally, financially, but, worst of all, in the time demanded—to include participation in city, state, national and international affairs. His whole existence is pulled further and further away from himself, until he almost loses his own identity in the sea of his affiliations.

Of course, this development has its positive aspects. When group activity is truly voluntary, it builds one of the most important bridges to the outside world, and counteracts the dangerous narcissism discussed before. But we have to understand that the specific structure of twentieth-century American society makes much activity compulsory, rather than voluntary, and forces everyone, time and time again, to participate in projects in which he is actually not at all interested.

The great danger of this enforced participation is most evident in an examination of the nature of social organization and personality in the communist world. This problem is not related to the relative merits of the capitalist and socialist economic systems or to the tremendous political pressure the Iron Curtain countries impose on their citizens. It derives from something else, from the extreme emphasis on the group, on group activity, on collective life, which almost inevitably reduces the individual to a kind of paralyzed loneliness. He can make no meaningful contact with others because he has neither the time nor the opportunity to become acquainted with himself, with his personal needs and his personal aims. Even when the goal of group activity derives from the highest motive— the urge to redeem the individual personality from loneliness—it defeats its own ends unless it simultaneously provides some degree of emotional fulfillment on the intimate, personal level. If it does not, it dooms the individual to isolation and loneliness, more intense because he is always surrounded by others.

These dangers are blossoming in our own country like some noxious weed. There are the suburban developments, row on row of identical houses occupied by identical families. There are the community centers and schools with their emphasis on group, rather than individual, activities. There is the lack of a private life, which is as deadly in the small towns as is impersonality in the big cities. There is the obsession with conformity and uniformity and adjustment. One *must* dress in a particular way, *must* have certain kinds of friends, *must* marry a certain kind of person, *must* adhere to certain political and artistic opinions. Under these circumstances, the rise in delinquency should come as no surprise; it is at least partially a reaction against the stifling social mold into which we force our children. And does all this collectivism help to overcome loneliness? Hardly. It proves only the courage of despair.

Paradoxically, this enforced participation is paralleled by an enforced isolation which can bring the most tragic consequences, for young people in this conformist culture frequently find it difficult to make friends among their contemporaries and to meet that one other person with whom they can build a bridge away from loneliness.

A young girl arrives in New York City from out of town. She has no acquaintances, no ties in the city. How is she to go about building a new life for herself? If she is not fortunate enough to meet congenial companions at her place of work, she faces a serious problem. The pattern of American cultural life is much more rigid in this area than is the European; in Paris or Berlin such a girl might spend an evening in one of the cafés, and no one would find it either unusual or reprehensible if she should strike up an acquaintance with the young man at the next table. Here, such behavior would put her outside the pale; Americans frown on the "pickup." Indeed, they tend to treat sheepishly the entire problem of how boy meets girl, and to leave it in the hands of middle-aged women of doubtful reputation or to the newspaper advertisements, with all their connotations of lecherous obscenity. At public dances, many sensitive young people feel like cattle on the auction block; they are so embarrassed, ashamed and humiliated that they may retreat into isolation rather than run the risk of rejection. Time and again I hear the same question, plaintive or angry, "How can I ever meet anyone I might marry?"

This is not just a personal matter, it is truly a social responsibility, and it is to be hoped that some group, or even the community itself, especially in the large cities where the problem is most acute, will take it out of the hands of the "professionals" and open meeting places that will guarantee a decency and wholesomeness that has heretofore been buried in the muddy, ugly atmosphere of the "lonely hearts clubs."

Between the pressures to conform and belong and the obstacles against the simplest kind of belonging—a belonging between two persons—more and more men and women tend to retreat into isolation and loneliness. For the pressures are severe; our civilization is compulsive and perfectionist. Things have to be done in a certain way or not at all. One must subscribe to certain ideas and to certain behavior. One must lose his individuality, and must imitate the false ideals which themselves are social products.

The most admired group in our culture seems to be "café society," this useless gang that moves in a pernicious atmosphere of drinking and promiscuity, with its snobbish exclusiveness, its wealth, its pseudo-knowledge and pseudo-culture. Its comings and goings, its witless remarks that

masquerade as wit, its marriages, divorces, affairs and business dealings are made public property by the gossip
columnists and press agents who can "make or break" any
well-known name. All this is part of the unholy business of
advertising and public relations.

Everybody takes it for granted that advertisements do
not mean what they say. No one believes that this soap, that
food, this medicine, that automobile, this comedian or that
candidate for public office is the best and only one to buy.
The aura of immorality that surrounds the sale of gasoline
and human beings, cheese and ideas is accepted and acknowledged; advertising has become deliberate falsification
based on specialized psychological research and scientific
ingenuity. Deceptions are repeated over and over until they
are accepted as truth, and ceaselessly our eyes and ears are
overpowered and raped by this noisy display. It cannot be
escaped, and gradually, unknowingly, we begin to yield.
Our judgment has been deliberately deranged, and we become part of still another group: consumers, united with
one another by the fact that all of us have been swindled
and tricked, duped and sucked into all kinds of diversions
from ourselves by a society which seems to be dedicated to
confusion, rather than to truth.

Ultimately, the individual must rebel against all this. He
cannot digest everything he is asked to swallow: the mass of
information and misinformation, the adulation of quantity
as opposed to quality. Although he may seem to conform
and even to welcome the restrictions and deceits of his culture, deep inside he knows that he is hopelessly caught and
hemmed in by laws, rules, regulations, conventions and organizations from which he cannot run away.

The sense of pressure is so severe, tension and anxiety
are so prevalent, that even the "normal" citizen feels im-

pelled to escape. This at least in part accounts for the fantastic current sale of the new tranquillizing drugs: In 1956 Americans spent almost fifty million dollars for two brands (Miltown and Equanil) alone. Apparently, large numbers of people prefer drowsiness and disinterest to the feeling that they are being chased and pushed by forces—from within and from without—over which they have no control.

Can the individual then refuse to be a part of his civilization? Can he simply reject a world that is unbearably painful, thwarting and frustrating? The ancient legend tells of Hercules, who was given a shirt as a gift. When he tried to take it off, his skin burst into flames, and he burned to death.

Jean Jacques Rousseau proposed a return to nature, and called on man to throw off all the artificial demands of his society. A few courageous souls have actually done it. The painter Gauguin deserted his wife, his family, his friends—his entire culture—lived briefly and died in a paroxysm of loneliness amid the glowing colors of Tahiti's gigantic flowers, its green trees and the dazzling nakedness of its bronze golden women. But such heroic and truly tragic decisions can be made by only a few. And the price they pay is high—too high.

Gauguin, transplanting himself from one culture to another, died in torment. I was once involved in an equally dramatic event, which could easily have had the same result.

A young Syrian woman had attempted suicide. I went to her apartment expecting to find a swollen, blue face, white lips and the sound of screaming and sobbing in an untidy room—all the distasteful accompaniments of a suicide attempt. Instead, Tanyi was sitting up in her snow-white bed, her slim, fragile, dark beauty clad in an oriental outfit, her slender brown legs in blue satin trousers crossed, Buddha-like, under her. A kind of thousand-and-one-nights atmosphere pervaded the clean, darkened, quiet room, and the exquisite girl could have been a character out of one of Scheherezade's tales. Tanyi's immense, translucent eyes were fixed straight ahead of her; she stared through me as if I did not exist. She was under an enormous emotional strain; some shock had brought her to the verge of losing contact with the world. This was a true emergency. Something radical had to be done, and quickly.

I speculated that such an abrupt retreat into complete isolation is usually the result of an experience of such painful content and dimensions that the ego loses its balance and trust in its own value, and simply denies the existence of the outside world. Were I to succeed in giving Tanyi back the reality she had lost by persuading her that I needed her, even in a small and trivial matter, I might be able to break through the dangerous barrier.

"I just lost a button from my jacket," I started innocently and without any introduction. "It looks awful. Do you think you could sew it on for me?" This tricky platitude, which played on her maternal impulses and put me in the position of a weak and vulnerable child, worked like magic. A tiny smile broke through the stony desert of Tanyi's face, and a few minutes later, while sewing on the button, the tears streaming down her cheeks, she sobbed out a story whose outlines, at least, I had suspected.

She had come to this country two years before with her husband, a brutal, brilliant and sensuous egotist who, brought up in the old Syrian tradition as she herself had been, had made her into one of his possessions. As it happened, the American atmosphere and culture attracted and captivated Tanyi, and when her husband decided to go back to Damascus, she refused to accompany him. He was enraged, and before flying home, he sent her a letter, which arrived as she was eating her breakfast the next morning. In it he stated, with shocking directness, that she was no longer his wife, that from this moment on, they were divorced. Tanyi had forgotten that the Syrian law gave him the right to this barbaric act.

Left alone, too ashamed to turn for help to the few of her countrymen who lived here, Tanyi faded away in absolute loneliness. Apparently, she had unconsciously counted on her husband and on her marriage, even though she and he were separated by thousands of miles and were living in entirely different worlds. Too timid and too stubborn to walk over the bridge that would bring her to real participation in the new culture, she refused the many marital offers which her strange and unusual beauty brought her. Rather, she indulged in lonely fantasies of sadistic murder and destruction of her husband until she could no longer contain her pent-up hate and finally turned all this horror against herself. It took many months to build her up again and to adjust her to the new life she had tried to throw away in lonely desperation.

Not everything must spell tragedy, and the problem of adjustment and of blending two different cultures into one can eventually be solved. I have always believed that the amalgamation of the European stock with the civilization of this country has produced a special brand of new and unique values, and one usually finds that the men and women who came here from abroad feel happier and more fulfilled than they did in their earlier days.

But even the more poignant incongruities of race can eventually be bridged. S. is an Indian, who like many of

his contemporaries was brilliant and highly gifted. He is
a member of that generation that grew up in New Delhi,
or on one of the fabulous estates of the countryside, and
studied at Oxford or Cambridge. He knows more about
European literature and art, and is a more perspicacious
critic of social and political currents than nearly anyone
I know.

One night when we were sitting and talking together,
my mouth on fire from all the sharp red and yellow tidbits
he had offered his guests for dinner, I succeeded in challenging him to a conversation about his philosophical
credo: "Every thought you think, every deed you do,
changes the world in some way."

"That's a bit paranoid, isn't it?" I prodded him.

"Maybe," he retorted, unruffled.

"Aren't you afraid of such a responsibility?"

"We grew up with it." He shrugged.

"But how did you manage, with such beliefs, to become
one of the world's great statesmen? You must, after all,
look at the world with a keen sense of reality if you are to
perform a diplomatic job properly."

He only smiled, but I got his answer a few days later,
when he invited a few friends, Indians and Americans, to
attend a showing of a film depicting his marriage the year
before to a maharani, a beautiful Indian princess, who
was one of the wealthiest women in the world.

While the film ran, S. sat on the floor beside my chair.
He wore a gray business suit, a white shirt and a subdued
tie. He was in high spirits and offered a running com-
mentary on the story as it unfolded before us on the screen.

"Here you see the front of my palace—half a mile long.
Here I am sitting on an elephant, getting seasick. That man
with the fancy white feather and the jewels all over his

breast—that's me. . . . Here my wife and I walk solemnly three times around the fire. . . . It's an ancient rite, and everything that follows represents some sort of symbolic something, too."

He went on this way for about half an hour, poking fun at himself—or rather at the man on the screen.

"Which of the two are you now?" I asked him when the film was over, "this man here in his American business suit, quite sophisticated, if you don't mind my saying so, or the other man over there on the screen?"

Again an amused smile lit up his face and, laying his hands on my shoulders, he replied: "You as a psychoanalyst, my friend, I'm sure know best that man lives simultaneously on different levels."

"Yes, I know it and you know it." I replied. "But you're actually living it. . . ."

We both laughed. But when I left, as I walked slowly down the broad stairs, I mused: "These Indians—maybe from them will spring the light that will shine into our darkness."

For the cultures of the East may be backwards when examined from a point of view that measures life's value exclusively in terms of washing machines and automobiles, streptomycin and atomic energy. But Western culture is equally backwards when it is seen in terms of the human personality, its needs and its nature. The Western world has rushed so fast into technical advance, nations and peoples tumbling over one another in the quest for material progress, that it has almost forgotten the only real purpose that can ever justify the frantic rush, the only real grail to be found: the hope of helping man to live together with his fellow men and in harmony with his own basic inner structure and requirements.

The long centuries during which the Eastern cultures slowly came to flower have produced a people mature enough to take in their stride the marvels that modern science and technology have made available to them, and to use these tools for man's true good. If the West can take a lesson from the East, if it can once again root itself in a deep appreciation both of man and of his society, twentieth-century man may finally be able to cope with the problems the age of anxiety has produced.

❖

CHAPTER THREE

The Vault of Communication

IN THE LAST few years strange reports have been trickling in from widely scattered radio stations and from amateur radio operators, who claim that they have, on more than one occasion, received radio signals which they could neither understand nor trace back to any transmitting station here on earth. The implication is that these signals originate in outer space, that they are being sent to us from other planets, that life exists in other parts of the universe, not just on earth alone.

Such a suggestion evokes more than simple scientific curiosity. It is both frightening and reassuring; frightening because nobody knows what this unknown life may be like and what its existence may mean for our futures, and reassuring because it indicates that we are not alone and that the mysterious strangers who may live on other planets are following one of life's oldest and most universal impulses: to break the circle of isolation in which all living things are enclosed by throwing a bridge of sound across the millions of miles of empty, freezing ether. If the reports are true, it would appear that the drive to communicate has been vital enough to smash all the obstacles and barriers that separate man from the rest of the universe.

Communication is indeed a prime need. Beginning with the lowest lumps of uncomplicated cell protoplasm and moving up on the sliding scale which culminates in man, all animal life displays this urge. Even the amoebas seem to make contact with one another, probably on the basis of a biochemical affinity. But such an explanation does not really tell us much about what actually takes place; biochemical affinity" are only words, labels for a process which is still not completely understood. Nevertheless, the process of mutual exchange and interchange does take place, and from this simple origin, it ascends in a more and more complex stratification and evolution.

Studies of the social organization among bees indicate that these insects have a complicated set of signals by which they can let one another know when a stranger breaks into their empire, can call on one another for help in carrying out the dead or bringing food into the hive, and can convey to one another the great news that the queen is ready to go on her mating flight.

Birds, too, have a communication system. How else are we to account for the fact that all at once whole flocks gather together for a flight to a warmer climate, under the direction of a single leader? Every day at the same time hundreds of pigeons hold a kind of town meeting on a particular tree in New York's Central Park, which I can see from the window of my office. All of a sudden, with a whirring of wings, they come together, fluttering and gossiping, interrupting whatever they may have been doing before, to sit crowded together on the branches, almost immobile. As I watch them, it is spectacularly evident that some kind of message is being transmitted among them. Is it exchange of the latest news of good food or breeding places? Are they deliberating as to who should be leader next spring and who secretary? Why do they pick this particular tree and how does each one of them know that, flying there, he will meet the others? Nobody knows. Nobody understands, as yet, the pigeon's language or how they "talk" to one another. But it seems obvious that they have some kind of communication system.

Recently, Norbert Casteret, in his book *The Descent of Pierre Saint Martin*, described his studies on the habits and modes of existence of the bats who make their homes in the great caverns of Southern France, near the Spanish border. In a fascinating account he records the experiments of two naturalists at Harvard University, Griffith and Galumbos, who, with the aid of an electronic apparatus called the ultrasonic analyzer, "showed conclusively that bats, when in flight, emit ultra-sounds whose frequency is of the order of 50,000 vibrations per second, i.e., that each 'cry' of communication lasts rather less than two hundredths of a second.

"A relatively spacious larynx equipped with powerful muscles causes these very high-pitched sounds. They are inaudible to man. . . . The bat is beyond all doubt equipped with radar, if we understand that word in its general sense as meaning the location of waves by echo. . . . Both the transmitting and the receiving apparatus appear to be extremely complex; but the principal facts are clear and it is not unlikely that nature may one day reveal other secrets of this kind, which are as yet unexplored and even unsuspected."[1]

Many years ago, I toyed with the idea of writing a book about animals, and for this reason obtained a special permit from a zoo director, which permitted me to visit the huge establishment whenever I wanted. I noticed that during the day, when the public flocked to see them, the animals

[1] Norbert Casteret, *The Descent of Pierre Saint Martin,* New York, The Philosophical Library, Inc., 1956 (page 147).

behaved quite unnaturally. They seemed disturbed, and paced restlessly back and forth in their narrow cages, apparently distressed by the constant staring, the noise and the teasing of innumerable small children and ignorant adults. The animals acted, in point of fact, just as would the species Homo sapiens under similar conditions. I decided, therefore, to do my research at night, when the great stillness had fallen on the city and everyone was asleep.

The zoo, too, was silent at this hour. Here and there an electric bulb cast its dim light over the cement paths and the shady lanes. The day's clamor was stilled, and as I walked along, I could hear the hollow echo of my steps. The birds sat motionless on their perches, their heads hidden deep in the warm featherballs of their tiny bodies. The lions, tigers, panthers and jaguars seemed to have forgotten their ferocity; they lay quiet and content. From time to time one of them would stir and thrust out a heavy paw. Perhaps he was dreaming happily of the kill, of fat and juicy lambs or tender white ducks.

Wandering at a leisurely pace from one silent cage to the next, I found myself in front of a vast enclosure. At that moment the moon came out from behind the fleecy clouds, and in the whitish blue mist I could distinguish a shape in that otherwise empty space: a dark, bulky mass, like a mountain. As I bent over the wooden fence trying to make out what it was, the mountain began to move, slowly and heavily, in my direction. It was a gigantic buffalo. I could see the legs, the massive body, the long brown hairs that fell over the clumsy, big head. The beast lumbered up and stopped right in front of me. His light blue eyes gazed searchingly for minutes into mine, with an expression of incredible loneliness and sadness. Somehow he was trying desperately to communicate some message to me. But I did not understand it. Or did I?

This sign language, that begins far down in the animal kingdom, leads past the fire signals of primitive man directly to the delicate nuances of poetry and literature and to the complicated modern means of communication: the telephone, the press, radio and television. And it will doubtless lead past these to the new inventions of the future.

Perhaps one day man will be able to establish some sort of meaningful contact with the life that may exist on those distant stars that are visible only as luminous dots in the night sky. Perhaps even before he can talk with them face to face, he will be able to make a living contact of give and take with these unknown "transmitters." But to do this, the messages they may be sending will have first to be deciphered.

"Decipher"—in that word is summed up half of the great challenge of human existence: the challenge of establishing contact and communion outside oneself, so that the conquest of loneliness can be achieved. For not only do all beings have the need to communicate, to extend themselves beyond the boundaries of themselves, they also have the need to understand that which is communicated to them, to become part of the world beyond themselves. And one needs more than language to enter this world of "the other." For man speaks with much more than his words; he speaks with equal eloquence through his gestures, his expression, his tone of voice, his carriage. All of these are essentially expressions of the unconscious, which open a door to undertanding the personality of the human transmitter. At the same time they give color, meaning and nuance to that which he transmits. A psychiatrist should be able, when a patient enters his office, to make a part of his diagnosis—the most important part—before that patient utters a single word. So many clues are hidden in so many trivial things: the way a man walks, his posture, whether he is rigid, hesitant or agitated; whether he slouches; whether his dress is carefully and deliberately arranged or is sloppy and shows the typical "I-don't-care" attitude; whether he looks straight ahead or shifts his eyes unsteadily without focussing on anything. Through such clues, such unconscious gestures, much more can be perceived than the consciously directed word expresses. Feelings of anxiety, contempt, jealousy, love or concern may come to the fore even though the speaker tries carefully to hide them behind the wall of his words. One unconscious communicates involuntarily with the other and speaks with a deeper impact and a deeper truth than any word can ever convey. It is for this reason that the psychoanalyst learns at least as much about his patient's character and ways of dealing with his difficulties at their first meeting as he does through the patient's later statements during treatment.

This same sensitivity to nonverbal communication can be attained by anyone who registers carefully and intently all the subtle manifestations of personality unconscious movements convey. Infants have a seismographic sensitivity; almost from the moment of birth they are aware of the real meaning behind their mother's words and gestures. The tone of her voice, the touch of her hand, the warmth of her body, the expression of her face—through these she communicates all her feelings to her child: her love or her resentment, her acceptance or her aggression, her warmth or her rejection. And the baby deciphers her meaning with an almost uncanny accuracy.

As everyone knows, this nonverbal communication is equally evident in lovers, who have an almost mysterious closeness, achieved not only through their eyes and the intimate contact of their bodies, but because their antennas are tuned to the same wave length: they speak silently to one another in a language which needs neither words nor the human voice. It is a kind of short circuit in which no spiritual or emotional girders are needed to span the chasm between the I and the You.

Of course, any kind of communication, even nonverbal communication, depends on the muscles and the motor system in general for transmission, and on the five senses for deciphering. And even more basically, it is a function of the anatomical structure that lies behind the muscles and the senses: the nerves that activate the muscles, the retina of the eye, the optic nerve of the brain, the tympanum of the ear, the acoustic lobe of the brain. The more developed these structures, the more subtly can they function and the greater are the possibilities both for communicating and deciphering. But communication has a psychological aspect as well. It depends on two basic suppositions which all communicating beings make: that those to whom one wishes to communicate have the same senses and that everyone experiences the events of the world in the same way; that what is to one a fragrant yellow flower is a fragrant yellow flower to the other as well.

These limitations on communication seem to be too severe for some people to accept; not satisfied with the miracle of life as it is, the miracle that permits the deep communion towards which all life aspires, they think they have discovered special means of communicating and deciphering that operate beyond the range of the motor system and the sensory organs. They call this phenomenon "extrasensory perception," and claim that telepathy and thought transference are realities. The experiments that have been performed in support of these claims have such a small margin of success that they actually prove nothing at all; nevertheless, the claims are made and argued passionately and vociferously. But even granted that such influences are theoretically conceivable, the question arises: why should only certain people, so-called mediums, be gifted with telepathic abilities denied to the rest of the human race? The experiments themselves seem to be of less significance than the need the experimenters show, despite man's rapid cultural development or rather, precisely because of it, to look for more and still more dramatic ways of breaking down the walls of isolation and loneliness in which he feels himself immured.

All children believe in magic; it performs many functions for them, not the least of which is the function of surmounting loneliness, of making contact with the incomprehensible and all-powerful forces that rule their lives. It is expected, however, that they will give up this belief when they reach the threshold of maturity. But many people remain attached to magic all their lives. Unable to make satisfactory contact with the world through natural means, or to find security and assurance in themselves and their relationship with others, they call on impersonal powers outside themselves for the strength they themselves lack. It seems to me that this is one of the reasons not only for the current interest in extrasensory perception, but also for the growing and naïve trust in all sorts of mediums, wonder-healers and others who are described as having supernatural powers. There is something tragic in all these childlike beliefs, these special miracles designed to add wonder and security to life. For the very existence of the world is enough of an eternal wonder and, despite all the scientific explanations, will remain an inexplicable and supreme enigma in itself. And so is man, and his ability to transcend himself by interacting with his world. He is and always will remain a miracle.

Of all man's ways of relating himself to his environment and of communicating with it, of all the bridges he builds away from himself to the other, language, with all its limitations, is obviously one of the safest, best functioning and most developed. Although its origins are lost in the mists of time, speech must have begun when primitive man first discovered that, in addition to the bodily gestures and facial grimaces by which he could express and communicate lust, desire, hunger, hate, sorrow and tenderness—the whole gamut of emotions—he could produce a scale of varying sounds by changing the vibrating resonance of his palate, tongue and lips as he let a stream of breath pass through his vocal cords. This is not the place to go into the details of this fascinating linguistic development; it followed a definite pattern, which has been traced by philology.

This book, however, is not concerned with language as sound, but as a tool which both satisfies the need to communicate, and which, in its use, reflects its user. The vernacular of New York's Lower East Side, the chitchat of two Bronx women, and the nightly colloquies of Greenwich Village intellectuals sound almost as if they were spoken in different languages; on the professional plane are the various jargons expressive of the worlds of sports, advertising, journalism, crime, medicine, etc. Socrates said, "Speak, that I may see you."

Still all these boundaries and barriers, difficult as they may sometimes be to overreach, are of much less significance than the general longing for communication and mutual understanding; they merely represent the variety that gives language its richness and flexibility. The intrinsic drive to communicate, to break the shell which encases each individual, remains the common denominator that unites all the shades and gradations of the human race.

Language is the most appropriate instrument with which man can satisfy his need to communicate with the outside world and thus conquer his loneliness, and therefore it is usually thrown away from the self and sent out towards the other; to inform him, to teach him, to threaten, caress or excite him. But it does not always have this function; language may be only secondarily communicative; speech can be directed inward, narcissistically, towards the speaker.

I remember myself, at the age of eight or ten, luxuriating in the warm water of my bath, shouting out verses and nonsense syllables at the top of my lungs, listening in delight as the sounds echoed back wildly from the high tile walls of the bathroom. All children use language in this fashion, it does not become primarily a communicative tool until about the sixth year of life. At first, children talk just for the sheer joy of talking, for the pleasure of hearing their own voices, for the fascination of feeling the words rising up in their throats and forming on their lips. This autistic use of speech is normal in the young child; he is still in the "oral stage," during which most of his psychological, emotional and sexual gratifications are experienced through his mouth. For it is through sucking at his mother's breast that the baby establishes his first contact with the outside world. At the same time, this sucking, in itself, assuages the infant's tormenting feeling of hunger and thirst. Displeasure and tension are thus changed into pleasure, the warm milk streams from one body into the other, and the baby falls asleep, peaceful and satisfied. In the broadest sense, then, we might call the pleasure the infant derives from sucking a sexual one, his first primitive gratification. For this reason the mouth retains a certain sexual function in later adult life; eating, smoking, talking, all these activities still have an element of their original sexual overtones. These will show most fatefully if for some reason the child, in the process of growth, has been prohibited from turning most of his sexual energy to the genital organs.

This narcissistic oral regression to a stage of early infantile sexuality is often noticeable in the speech of underdeveloped children. It also remains a component, although a minor one, in the speech of many adults, as well. The orator, the political speaker and the actor all derive a very real pleasure from their own muscle movements, from the sound and rhythm and beauty of their words; this enjoyment is often an important unconscious factor in their choice of vocation, just as important as their conscious delight in communicating with others and conveying information or emotion. Many distinguished public figures seem to taste every word and sentence they utter, to roll each one around in their mouths with enormous gusto, before they finally allow it to trespass the threshold of their dental fences. If this narcissistic self-enjoyment overrides the adult's desire to communicate, to build a bridge away from himself, it can be safely assumed that something is decidedly wrong with his emotional health.

The red-haired, freckled, highly gifted schizophrenic girl talked incessantly. During her therapeutic sessions she would invent certain phrases of rare poetic beauty and rhythm and repeat them over and over again. She was drunk with words, caressed and tasted every one of them in her large, red-lipped mouth. She knew that she was not really interested in the content of her speech; that, indeed, her utterances made very little sense; any meaning in them was only accidental. Nor did she really care much whether or not I understood what she was saying. What she wanted most was the pleasure of making the sounds and listening to their rhythm.

Among the technological wonders that have expanded man's world of communication, the telephone has an intrinsically symbolic role. The automobile, the train and the airplane have contributed substantially to broadening the radius of man's experience in space; the telephone, standing inconspicuously on the desk, does something more vital: it makes it possible for the individual to throw his voice and his thoughts anywhere in the world. Now everyone can speak into everyone else's ears, and in addition, each man must keep his own ears open, willy-nilly, to anyone who wants to shout or whisper into them. This ingenious little machine, one of the most marvelous of all devices for overcoming loneliness, has in many cases become instead a cruel and uncompromising master, whose vulgar and relentless ring commands the individual to interrupt whatever he may be doing or thinking, and to make himself available not only to important messages, but to the most foolish and trivial ones as well.

In addition, it has opened wide a door to a shocking emotional regression. Certain people—usually women—exploit the telephone only as a tool for infantile oral sexual gratification; it provides them with a chance to babble unrestrainedly for hours. Their conversation has no real content; it consists of an endless accumulation of small talk, of backbiting, of the latest gossip, of a detailed accounting of meaningless nonsense. To the trained listener it is evident that these prolonged orgastic excesses are not even intended to create mutual contact and communication; they serve only as easy ways to release pent-up aggression and to derive narcissistic enjoyment.

For a whole month a middle-aged woman telephoned me every night to tell me, in detail, that I was a piece of dirt, the son of a something, a rotten apple dangling from a warped tree, a thief and a murderer. She was drunk, and cursed happily for an entire hour, usually from two to three A.M. She did not expect me to answer her attacks, she neither knew nor cared whether she woke me up, whether I was alone when she called, nor how I felt about her verbal onslaughts. She was getting rid of her own aggressions and the violent hate she had transferred from her childhood and had cheerfully preserved until late in her adult life. She did not intend to hurt me, personally; her attack was levelled against her parents, who had treated her badly as a child. And she felt relieved and considerably better each time she gave herself this colossal relief, and each time enjoyed a good, sound, innocent sleep as soon as she hung up.

Teen-agers provide another glaring example of this kind of telephonic release. The stream of words is emitted with a kind of hectic eagerness and irrelevance which calls to mind the undirected method of free association, used deliberately and to good purpose in psychoanalysis, but applied here to no therapeutic purpose at all. Nearly always the faces of the transfixed speakers show a kind of narcissistic bliss, and usually their conversations end with the assurance, "I'll call you again later," a promise of another boundless discharge of condensed self-pleasure!

One additional factor makes this telephonic intercourse

so attractive to many people and lures them into wasting
their precious time: the fact that their partner is invisible.
The speaker is alone with his strange device; the other
person is, in a sense, only imagined, only his voice identifies him. Under such circumstances it is not too surprising
that the very limitations of the situation become an unusual
temptation for those who are afraid to experience reality
as it is, and who see it only as the product of their own
imaginations. It is interesting to speculate as to the manner
in which this eerie communication will change and lose its
narcissistic quality at the not-too-distant time when science
will develop an electronic device by which the other person
will not only be heard, but seen as well. It seems that in
certain situations man actually prefers to leave a part of
reality to his imagination. If this were not the case, radio
would have become obsolete as soon as television was invented. And the factor of anonymity is doubtlessly even
more significant in the case of an instrument that gives the
individual a chance not only to be on the active transmitting end, but on the receiving and deciphering end as
well.

For people do not always speak. Sometimes they listen.
And here, too, the question of communication versus narcissism comes into play. Not only must the speaker want
to communicate, the listener must want to decipher, must
want to make a real contact. He must want to surround
and absorb the words, emotions and ideas that come to him,
so that he can expand his self-boundaries and thus enrich
his life. He must approach this emotional food of communication as the amoeba approaches the microscopic
motes on which it feeds, by flowing around them, engulfing
them and making them a part of itself. For whether a man
is the speaker or the listener, the actor or the audience, the

writer or the reader, whether he produces a television show or watches it, he is engaged in communicative activity. In all these means of extended communication, as in private conversation, each member of the audience has a choice: either he can make a true contribution to his own growth and to the conquest of loneliness by incorporating the ideas, feelings and emotions, the tragedies, problems, conflicts and joys to which he is exposed, or he can use them in a narcissistic way, to blow up his own self-pity and to increase the self-imposed misery from which he derives a masochistic enjoyment.

The press, radio and television have an immense psychological influence on modern man. Since their invention he has become a participant not only in the sufferings and the laughter of those who are in fact part of his life, with whom he shares the same home or the same office, but in the fate, the accidents, the catastrophes, the births and deaths, revolutions and wars, loves and hates and joys of millions of others, thousands of miles away. He may react to this constant barrage of information by learning to identify with those whose lives have now become a part of his own, by expanding his capacity to receive, to decipher and to communicate, so that the new media become bridges away from himself to the world, or, on the other hand, he may feel as if he is standing convulsed in fear, on his own tiny island, in the middle of a limitless sea whose ceaseless waves pound relentlessly against the rocky coast defenses of his shrinking ego. With this in mind, it becomes even easier to understand how devastating is the impact on the individual of our contemporary "quiz kid" and "sixty-four-thousand-dollar question" civilization, with its emphasis on quantity rather than quality. It is almost impossible for anybody to digest all the information that comes thundering towards him at every moment, and to grasp its full extent and meaning, if, indeed, it has any real meaning. It sometimes seems as if man gathers all these words and facts only in order to piece them together into a kind of flimsy spiritual garment, designed to cover his emptiness and his sense of fear and loneliness.

One evening my telephone rang.

"I need psychoanalysis," a man's voice said, curtly and without any introduction.

"You do?" I answered, wondering.

The next day, at the prescribed time, the man behind that voice arrived. He opened the office door and marched, silently and without looking at me, straight to the couch.

"I have an Oedipus complex," he said, lying down comfortably and evidently enjoying himself thoroughly.

"You have what?" I asked.

"I just told you. Aren't you a psychoanalyst?" he replied, a bit irritated.

"I don't know what I am." I smiled. "I haven't been in this country very long, and my English isn't very good. What are you talking about?"

"I love my mother," he blurted out peevishly.

"That's fine." I nodded. "What's wrong with that?"

Now he got truly upset and screamed, furiously: "And I'll kill my father!"

"You don't mean it," I said quietly. "Come, sit up."

Reluctantly, he did. Obviously he was musing about whether he ought not to leave me and take his Oedipus complex to a "true" analyst. It took him a whole year to learn what an Oedipus complex was and what the word psychoanalysis meant, for it was a year before he could break through the hard crust of words in which he had encased himself and feel the emotions from which his pseudoscientific vocabulary had protected him.

About the same time, perhaps a few weeks later, a hysterical girl lay on the same couch. I tried to listen to what she had to say, but I was diverted by the antics of a tiny baby mouse, which was running, fearsome and fidgety, around the room. It looked delightful in its light gray skin, trying to find something edible on the floor near the couch. My office happened to be situated in an old building, and although the house was kept immaculately clean one lonely mouse seemingly still had a chance. This skinny little animal apparently hoped to dig up something for his hungry stomach, or perhaps he was chasing around just for the fun of it. Whatever the reason for his adventure I must confess that he quite distracted me from giving my full attention to the girl on the couch, and I waited with anxious anticipation to discover what kind of explosion would occur when she saw the inoffensive little intruder.

When her hour was up, the girl got up from the couch.

"Look . . . look there," she whispered hoarsely, pointing at the mouse, who at that moment had decided to sit still and give himself a well-deserved rest.

"Yes?" I replied innocently.

"But it's a mouse," she stammered.

"Yes, it's a mouse," I reassured her mischievously.

"But it's a mouse," she screamed now.

"Yes, it's a mouse," I said, with some finality.

"But . . . but I thought mice were symbols," she rebelled, obviously bewildered and confused by her scientific knowledge.

"A mouse is a mouse before it becomes a symbol," I lectured her. Beyond the laughter I felt rising in my throat,

I noticed with dismay the dangerous degree of confusion that had spread and grown in the girl's disturbed brain.

This habit of substituting words for feelings, symbols for objects, intellectualization for emotion, is a very common one. It is not the analyst but the patient who loves to use psychiatric lingo during his sessions. Most often he thinks that all he need do to solve his problems is to pin labels on them.

The mistake is by no means confined to men and women who undergo psychoanalytic treatment. It is almost characteristic of our era; people use the tools technology has given them to run away from themselves, their lives and their loneliness, and often they use the greatest of all human tools—language—in the same way.

The main pipe through which our communication waters are pumped, under greater or less internal pressure, is, of course, conversation. When this pipe is clogged, when even simple conversation becomes difficult, loneliness becomes terror. What are the obstacles that have such an effect? First is the common complaint, "There's nobody to talk to." In other words, there is available no object worthy of receiving the messages we want to send out from the prisons of ourselves. In some situations that might be realistically true. Our culture does in fact erect walls to bar communication, especially between "strangers." But the actual social obstacles, strong as they may be, are in most cases of less importance than the self-created ones, those produced by the individual's own imagination, by his own concepts of himself and the world.

Here we approach the heart of the entire problem of loneliness, a disease which is, after all, basically a failure of communication in one or many areas. The neurotic and the psychotic, with their erroneous and unrealistic self-concepts and their distorted pictures of reality, are so frightened that they would rather suffer in their self-produced loneliness and isolation than communicate with the world and cope with the realities and problems of life. In the next chapters we will analyze in some detail the different forms this loneliness can take. Here I would like only to describe two especially enlightening situations.

The first concerns a six-year-old child, a chubby little girl with stiff brown pigtails. She was pretty, but anxious-looking; from time to time she squinted her round brown eyes. She had talked, although with a slight stammer, until about a year before. Suddenly, however, she had become completely mute. Several doctors had examined her. None had found anything organically wrong. But her speech had not returned.

The child did not come alone. She was accompanied by her mother, a tall, thin, drawn woman in her early thirties, the prototype of all the tense, unhappy, hectic, angry women whose dissatisfactions with life have made ugly imprints on their faces and show in every one of their movements. The disturbed relationship between mother and child was strikingly obvious. The mother tried to ignore her daughter; several times she pulled away from the child, who clung anxiously to the folds of her dress. Her apparent solicitude and concern were far from real, or she would not have tried to shake off her daughter with such impatient gestures. Her conversation began with a declaration of love for her "baby" and then turned into a complaint; she treated me to a long recital about the care she had lavished on this ungrateful creature, the sleepless nights she had spent, the energy she had invested, all the work and drudgery that had cost her her looks and her youth. This type of "sacrificing" mother is all too familiar to the psychiatrist. Although she constantly advertises all she has done and what a good mother she has been, the simple fact is that she does not love her child, and never wanted it in the first place. She does not like the responsibility of taking care of others; she would much prefer to be the child herself, so that others would have to take care of her. Although, as an atonement for her guilt feelings, she tries to hide her resentment and hate from herself and from the world behind a mask of exaggerated concern and love, her hostility is shown by her constant demand for gratitude and repayment.

After listening to the mother for a few minutes, I asked her to leave me alone with the child. She refused. It was her child. She knew best and she was not going to give her helpless baby into the hands of some "strange" doctor, who might, for all she knew, do the child harm. Insisting quietly that if she did not leave, I would not treat her daughter, I finally persuaded her to go.

Out of his vast clinical experience, Sigmund Freud prescribed that, in the first hours of treatment, the analyst should "seduce" his patient. I attempted this, but no matter how hard I tried, my efforts to create a contact with my little patient simply did not work. I joked with the child, I laughed, I grimaced, I cajoled. I crouched on the floor imitating a barking dog. Of course, I enjoyed myself with all these childish tricks, but none of them were of any avail. I simply made a fool of myself, and the child stared at me blankly. The only sign of any reaction at all was an increase in her nervous squinting, and, despite all my efforts, she remained obstinately mute.

From the moment mother and child had entered the office, I had felt that the key to the child's problem lay in the mother's behavior and the child's reaction to it, and it seemed to me that the girl would not regain her speech until she herself came to a basic understanding and acceptance of her feelings, without guilt. Normally, the patient acquires this understanding not through what the analyst tells him, but through his own emotional experience of himself and his feelings towards his analyst as he verbalizes them in treatment. But with a child, and one who would not talk, the usual analytic technique would not work. Obviously, something new and different had to be invented.

Months before, I had begun to work on a research project in psychotherapy in several of New York's hospitals. The technique consisted in having adult patients smear around with half-fluid colors on sheets of paper and then asking them to express verbally whatever came to their minds when they looked at their own work. This finger painting had been invented years before by a gifted school teacher, Ruth Faison Shaw, who had recommended it as an emotional outlet for disturbed children. In my work with adults, the finger painting became more than a mere occupational therapy; it was rather a kind of graphic psychoanalysis or dream analysis, in which the patient gave his free associations to the manifestations of his own unconscious.

Although I realized that I could not ask the little girl for any verbal interpretation of her work if I gave her finger paints to play with, it seemed to me that if I were to succeed in having her express her unconscious conflicts in her paintings, she might not only give needed clues to an understanding of her muteness—it was, of course, possible that my hypothesis was wrong—but in addition she might, with help and reassurance, achieve some understanding of these conflicts and become sufficiently excited and stimulated by her pictures to break the barrier of her voluntary retreat and isolation. Under these circumstances, she would be able to find her way back to an unblocked communication through language.

Since I assumed that the child's muteness was an expression of resentment against her demanding and unloving mother, I reasoned that if I were simply to ask the child to paint, she would probably refuse. It would seem to her that I was only repeating the pattern of her mother's behavior. I therefore took out some sheets of paper and the six containers of paint and began to paint.

"I'm a painter," I said to her. "If you don't mind, I'd like to work now. Make yourself comfortable. You can do anything you'd like."

I busied myself with the finger paints, seemingly paying no attention at all to the child. As I expected, her curiosity soon overcame her. Swinging her arms, she sauntered across the room and peeped over my shoulder to find out what I was doing. After a few moments, I suggested that she could join me if she wanted to and I laid out a piece of paper on the table near mine. She nodded, and began to paint, absorbed and eager. The first battle was won.

For the next two weeks she came every day and spent her hour painting away, without any interference from me. I sat at my desk and tried to give her the impression that I was doing my own work. The only comments I made were those that expressed my appreciation and respect for her work and talent. A smile was her first answer.

Then, one morning, when I was sure she knew I was her friend, I put all her paintings together in a row.

"Would you like me to tell you what I wonder about?" I asked her, looking at one painting after another.

She nodded.

"Well"—I examined the paintings carefully—"let's see." I held one in my hand. "This must be a battleship." I picked up the next. "And this one is an airplane crashing down on someone who was shooting at it. This one? Well, here are cannons and soldiers with swords and knives. . . ." I looked at the last painting she had done. "This one, where everything is red, that's blood, isn't it?"

Again she nodded, more slowly this time. She watched me earnestly and suspiciously out of the corner of her eyes.

"I think they're all beautiful. I couldn't have painted them any better myself." I smiled at her.

Now she was very tense. She licked her lips and I noticed with delight that she looked disappointed. The moment for the frontal attack had arrived.

"It occurs to me that you might want to kill someone," I said, with as much nonchalance as I could muster. "Maybe mother, or someone." And after a few seconds, "You really don't like her too much, do you? Sometimes I guess she is a bit hard to bear. I mean, it would be good just to have her out of the way for a while. What do you say?"

Suddenly, I swung around to face her, looking with affection straight into her eyes. She stared directly back into mine; for a moment all the blood went out of her face and she was ashy pale. Then her color came rushing back. A tiny twinkle grew in her wide-open eyes. We were accomplices, and her full lips stretched wide, responding to my acceptance and understanding with a broad, happy grin.

"See you tomorrow," I said. "That's all for today."

When she came the next morning it was hard for me to conceal my excitement, and although I had expected something of the kind I felt a bit shaky when she came towards me, extending a chubby hand and saying, triumphantly, in her clear, childish voice: "Good morning, Doctor."

"Your child is cured," I said to the mother a few minutes later. "Now it's your turn."

Obviously, if the mother was to persist in her bitter and rejecting behavior, the child might again retreat into muteness. Her silence and her refusal to communicate had been her only defense; she preferred loneliness and total isolation to the pain of contact with the outside world, which she saw as nothing but an extension of her mother.

The other example concerns a dream. This is not the place to describe in detail our knowledge of the structure and meaning of these nocturnal hallucinations. Examination of brain waves on the electroencephalograph has proved what we already knew: that the brain does not stop functioning during sleep, but continues to operate, although at a different level. What interests the psychoanalyst about the dream is something else: the fact that the moral censorship we call conscience is dulled during sleep. Consequently, the individual's hidden drives and repressed instinctual impulses come to the surface in his dreams. But because the conscience though tuned down is still active, these repressed wishes are usually veiled in fanciful symbolic garments, often so heavily embroidered that it appears as if the unconscious—that of which we do not want to be conscious—is battling violently to hide rather than to communicate its message, because of the load of guilt and fear associated with it.

In this dream communication the dreamer is a young woman. She is blonde and blue-eyed, and her exquisite face is masklike, almost immobile. With her fine features and delicate white complexion she reminds one of the statuary of one of the great Greek sculptors. And her graceful, long-limbed body is reminiscent of a young Diana. Her beauty is marred by only one thing: her lower lip is just a trifle too short, betraying a kind of frozen and sadistic cruelty. Her voice is low and monotonous, strangely devoid of warmth and feeling. She is highly intelligent, yet she wastes her time and her gifts in a petty job, unworthy of her talents. With all her unusual bodily beauty and her brilliance she has, nevertheless, retracted her emotional life to a dangerous degree; she is almost always oppressed by a feeling of terror, abandonment and lonely panic. And yet she has many friends, or at least people who call themselves her friends. As a matter of fact, she is constantly surrounded by a crowd of young men and women, a permanent stream with whom she wanders aimlessly from one cocktail party to the next. At each she is the center of attention, not only because of her beauty, but also because she is a charming clown. She seems to have embarked on a never ending quest straight into the hearts of mankind, and she will not rest until everyone is smitten with her, full of love and glowing admiration. But after every bedlam of seemingly delightful joy, she says good-bye to all the play-acting and goes straight home, to lie awake on her bed for hours in utter loneliness and misery. Or she allows one of the young men she has just met to take her up to her room, and she makes love to him in a hard, desperate and aggressive shamelessness, waiting hopelessly to receive the affection she herself cannot give and consequently is given only in passionate fractions.

This young woman's childhood was badly marred. Her father was a deeply disturbed man; he beat his daughter unmercifully, not for her misdeeds, but because of his own emotional problems. The mother, instead of protecting her against these sadistic outbursts, actually encouraged them because she had been jealous of her child from the very moment of its birth. The girl was dazed, totally unable to comprehend a life in which her need for love was so constantly and so savagely cut off. She knew absolutely no way to relate to anyone; it is therefore not surprising that she should have withdrawn into a confused hate and isolation. On her sixteenth birthday she courageously left home and soon thereafter she gave herself in thoughtless hate to the first man who wanted her. Even when she became aware of the power of her unusual beauty, she was still unable to give up her deadly distrust and suspicion of men. It seemed to her that all the admiration so freely given her was only a trick designed to bring the man sexual satisfaction. Her life seemed to be draining away in one empty conquest and triumph after another, until finally it became nothing but a glistening chain of suffering, which she enjoyed with a deeply masochistic self-debasement. As if to prove something to herself, she went through several marriages, none of which lasted for more than a short time. Finally she decided to seek help through psychoanalysis.

For the first few months she spent her hour still and motionless on the couch, her features unmarred in their tragic and waxlike beauty. And then came the dream which, with one abrupt and blinding stroke, enlightened the whole tragedy of this "glamorous" life.

"I dreamed I was in Italy," she almost whispered. "I was trying to speak to someone on the telephone, but I didn't know how to handle the apparatus. There was an old Italian woman sitting on the floor and I asked her, time and time again, in Italian, '*Scusi, signora,* couldn't you help me? I don't know how to work this telephone.' But she only shook her head as if she didn't understand what I was saying, although I knew I spoke good Italian. All this time, I was holding the receiver desperately to my ear. And then suddenly my mother's voice came through it, saying, very simply: 'Hello, darling, how are you?' She didn't seem surprised, nor was I, that she had reached me, speaking from somewhere in America to her daughter, somewhere in the middle of Europe."

It does not require professional knowledge to recognize this as the convulsed cry of the child breaking through the grown woman's stony façade, now beginning to crumble. Out of the cellar of her unconscious the deeply repressed anxiety of the bewildered child had broken to the surface; the fear and terror of the crushed and lonely mind that does not know how to communicate with a strange world in whose language it cannot be understood even though it speaks clearly and distinctly. The uncomprehending Italian woman was an image of the mother, who had refused to understand her daughter even in her earliest days. And, as so often happens in dreams, the mother played more than one role, for her child thought of her in more than one way. Not only was she cruel and heartless, she was, in the dream, warm and loving as well, as her daughter had always wanted her to be. Out of the feeling of abandoned nothingness emerged the fulfillment of the child-woman's most secret wish: that she is not alone, that, contrary to the reality, a loving and ever present mother is reaching out to her with the simple question: "Hello, darling, how are you?"

With this story we approach the dark door through which all these poor souls pass who have chosen the false road of flight, escape and withdrawal from their self-imposed loneliness, the door on whose empty walls the wanderer reads the words that Dante wrote on the entrance gate to hell: *Lasciate ogni speranza, voi ch'entrate!* Or is there hope?

Part Two: The Defenses

CHAPTER FOUR

A Road Map of Escape

IN HIS FLIGHT from himself and his loneliness, man can travel a confusing maze of blind alleys and dead ends. Although these roads may appear quite different from one another, all of them are directed towards the same goal: escape from isolation. The search to find ramparts and defenses against pain is one of the intrinsic operating characteristics of the human mind. Often ingenious, it is always deceitful and unsuccessful, for it is aimed towards avoiding the causes of pain rather than facing them squarely so that they can be overcome.

These self-deceiving attitudes, by which black becomes white and truth falsehood, are called neurosis, and, when they are carried to an extreme, psychosis. Communication is blocked, more or less severely, and in his panic the individual does either one of two things. He may retreat into a paralyzing hate, into the delusion which sees hostility and anger as the only bridge to the other. Or he may regress into an infantile narcissism, into self-gratifying loneliness. The ego, overwhelmed by its suffering and unwilling to participate any longer in a world it sees as threatening and frightening, incarcerates itself in a prison of its own making and stares through the false and artificial safety of the prison bars at the bewildering life "outside." This escape from reality is, symbolically, a return to the mother's womb, a regression to the earliest stage of development, during which man is not yet alone and not yet lonely. Unwilling and unable to cope with the pitfalls and abysses of reality, the neurotic attempts to save himself by simply denying the existence of the realities he perceives. The alteration of values can be executed on a broad scale of shades and nuances, corresponding to the degree of severity of the emotional illness. To give in a single chapter a definitive account of the intricate and involved nature and dynamics of mental disease is almost impossible; such a treatment cannot be anything but superficial. Still neurosis presents such an intrinsic part of the human defense system against loneliness that it could not possibly be omitted from this book. Thus the reader will have to accept a condensed simplification of psychodynamic mechanisms which are in actuality extremely complex.

At the bottom of the run-away processes, on the first rung of the slippery ladder, is the imposter. He cannot tolerate being himself because he cannot accept his real or self-induced loneliness, and so he tries to persuade himself, that he is someone else. There is usually something clownish in his behavior; he shows a certain childishness which paradoxically enough actually represents his distorted wish to acquire the glamor he sees in parenthood. Since he perceives himself as an eternal child, he has never been able to reach this fancied maturity.

Every child has the imposter's tendency to play-act. Watch a little girl with her doll. It is easy to see that she alternately plays the role of the mother and the baby; she is both the mother she would like to have and the child she would like to be. If she fondles her doll, it is because she wants to be loved and caressed herself. If she beats it, she is trying to atone for and expiate her own misdemeanors, real or imagined. This childish play-acting, this enjoyable and often humorous behavior, forms the basis for any kind of acting at all, from the simplest to the most sophisticated. As an escape, it is disastrous. But properly used, it can represent one road towards redemption from a lonely existence.

When I was a young medical student, I spent a summer vacation in the French Alps. One day I was standing in front of the little chalet above the famous Mer de Glace, near Mont Blanc, chatting with two of the tough and silent mountain guides, when a middle-aged couple, typical petty bourgeois from Saxony, approached.

"Any of you guys get us over the glacier?" the rotund husband asked. "We're toughies, mamma, ain't we?" He gave his buxom wife a resounding smack across her well-upholstered bottom.

"Yes, sir," I said on a sudden impulse, checking quickly to see if there was a sanctioning twinkle in the eyes of my companions.

Down we went on the ice, jumping over the cracks and crevices. I answered my charges' foolish questions with even more foolish answers, and enjoyed myself enormously by pretending to be relatively unfamiliar with their language, which, of course, I knew perfectly well.

"Could I tempt you to have a bite of mamma's homemade liverwurst?" the chubby, red-cheeked woman panted as we climbed along.

"No, thank you," I declined in a broken German of my own invention. "We guides are not supposed to eat meat. Or vegetables. Or bread. We eat only *du sucre, toujours, toujours du sucre.* For energy, you know."

"But that's dreadful, that's really too bad." She took me

at my word and clucked sympathetically. "You're married, aren't you? Your wife . . ."

"I have no wife."

"You haven't? A nice-looking young man like you?"

"No, ma'am. Maybe if I'd met someone like you I'd have been tempted. But it wouldn't be fair. You wouldn't ever sleep. How would you feel, gracious madam, if you knew that your husband was exposed to danger every day, instead of working peacefully and safely in his store? No, madam, I couldn't do that to any woman."

And so it went, until we had traversed the glacier and arrived safely at the little restaurant on the other side.

"How much do we owe you?" the fat, sweating husband asked.

"Ten francs," I replied, by now a bit embarrassed at the trick I had played on them.

"Why don't you give him fifteen?" the wife spoke in a stage whisper into her husband's big, fleshy ear. "After all, he's such a good guide." She smiled at me coyly.

Back with my friends, the real guides, we transformed the fifteen francs, with roars of laughter, into glass after glass of bittersweet red chianti until we went to bed. A few hours later we got up again and went down to the ice. It was still dark. One of the men lit the candle in his lantern. The stars were trembling sparks. Not a sound broke the stillness. We tied the rope and climbed slowly and rhythmically up to the high plateau of Mont Blanc. The air grew thinner and the silence was interrupted only by the creaking of the snow under our heavy boots. The icy pinnacles became gray, gradually changing to violet, green and pink. At last the sun ball itself burst over the horizon in brazen glory.

It was the magnificent isolation of this frozen mountain

world, with its atmosphere of lonely splendor, that had prompted me to act as I did, to jump suddenly and laughingly out of myself to escape the suffocating embrace of empty space. Often the walls that separate health from pathology are thin indeed; it is not always easy to discover where one leaves off and the other begins.

Some jugglers play their lost games in just that no man's land. Such a one was George, an Englishman, small and chubby, who looked like one of those fuzzy teddy bears children love to play with and to fondle. Sitting on the floor, playing with children as though he was a child himself, George showed a warmth and affection, and an understanding of childhood and the child's mind that seemed anything but wrong. But in fact George was playing a neurotic role; being a child was his first and most genuine assumption of a part that was not himself. His behavior was less an act than an effort to achieve, as an adult, a childhood enjoyment he had never realized.

Next he became a painter and artist, but an artist of a peculiar brand. If he was asked for a picture in the style of Rubens, George would produce a painting that looked completely genuine. If he was in the mood to be Gauguin, the picture would be a Gauguin. Indeed, all of his forgeries were so skilled that an art expert would have found it extremely difficult to distinguish George's work from the work of the true master. This went on for some time, until he finally got tired of it, as any neurotic tires of his symbolic *quid pro quo* and has constantly to change it because it is irrational. One is reminded of the famous figure of Don Juan, whose compulsive philandering symbolically disguises his eternal quest to seduce and conquer his mother.

Next on George's playful road of escape from his own identity came the role of a famous *chef de cuisine,* a role he was able to assume with considerable success for some weeks, since his own infantile oral regression made it a particularly suitable part for him. But eventually the restaurant owner for whom he worked learned that George had never been a chef before, and dismissed him summarily. George was always driven by some unconscious need for punishment which led him to expose himself just when his position seemed most secure. But discovery never prevented him from continued play-acting, and his next role—for his ambition fed on itself—found him in the uniform of an English air marshal. Since there were at the time only two such gold-braided gentlemen in all of Britain, it was to be expected that George's glory would bloom only for a few days before he was found out. Yet by an ironic streak, he was never imprisoned or severely punished for his behavior. Each time he was unmasked, he was simply dismissed. Despite his unconscious wish for punishment, poor George always found himself charming his judges into a special act of clemency.

At last, offended fate caught up with him. He finally ran into a reality which, with all its tragic overtones, smashed into fragments his flimsy building of dreams and fantasy.

Shortly after the Second World War, he appeared in a little French village, posing as a former British liaison officer to the French underground. The mayor of the town, the notables and all the good citizens were overjoyed to meet him and thrilled to have a chance to honor the man who had helped to free them from the brutal Nazi yoke. They planned a celebration for him and, to give it a special touch of glamor, invited one of the leaders of their own French Maquis. When this simple and straightforward little man, who had actually risked his life for his country, and whose disfiguring scars bore testimony to the horrible wounds he had suffered, was introduced to the playful imposter, the pretense was shaken.

"I'm sorry," he said, "I've never seen this man before."

George silently left the festive table, loaded with the best of French food and wines—and killed himself. The road of escape was blocked, the play was over, and the curtain came down with a crash.

"To thine own self be true," Polonius said. But the neurotic is likely to answer: "How can I? I don't know what I am or what the true me is." For he does not dare to be himself. This was George's tragic omission.

A similar climate of fear and the tragedy of "too late" enveloped two young people who had met, dined and danced one evening in a mute mutual attraction, and whose lifeboats had then drifted in different directions. Seven years later they met again by chance, on an icy-cold gray morning in November in the unheated studio of a silly little Chinese photographer, who was taking pictures of them for the cover of a cheap magazine. They danced in the false pinkish light and sipped gingerale that was supposed to represent champagne. The girl wore an artificial rose on the elegant evening gown she had borrowed for the occasion and her partner was dressed in a rented tuxedo. As they went through the routine and prescribed act of make-believe love, their entwined bodies, without either their will or their knowledge, became enflamed by the fire of a passionate desire that, through all the empty years, had been simmering at the center of their lives.

"Why didn't you act this way seven years ago?" the girl

stammered desperately. "Why didn't you, instead of talking about horses all the time?"

The escape from loneliness through an attempt to be someone else is called identification. This form of the flight from isolation is a psychic phenomenon that operates, at least to some degree, in every human being, healthy or sick. In reading a book or seeing a play, it is natural to identify with that character towards whom one feels some kinship or whom one would like, in one's fantasies, to be. It is this human tendency that has created the fairy tale, in which real people do not exist, but only kings, queens, princes, princesses and evil fairies and in which Prince Charming always comes to the rescue of the innocent, poor and lonely maiden.

Is all of this neurotic? Hardly. As long as the individual is aware of what he is doing, as long as his day-dreaming does not actually begin to substitute for reality, identification helps him to conquer his loneliness by expanding his ego and his horizons, so that he can incorporate more and more of the outside world into himself. But at the moment his play-acting begins to blot out the real world, he retreats into emotional illness, more or less severe. Behind this sickness lies the child's conception that life is dangerous, that the world to which it has been so abruptly exposed after the security of its mother's womb is a terrifying threat. The most important single distortion in the reality life of the neurotic is that, regardless of the degree of his intellectual awareness, he still feels in childish terms. He never really understands that as an adult he is equipped with basically different weapons than is the child, and that, consequently, he can fight his own battles and win his own victories.

This retreat into the womb, this identification with early life, lies behind nearly all the sick emotional patterns the psychoanalyst sees daily in his patients. It is both the result and the repetition of the patient's childhood behavior, which itself developed as a way of escaping from loneliness and from painful experiences into a happier world of the imagination. But the neurotic does not realize that his behavior actually increases the loneliness from which he is trying so desperately to escape. Always he sees himself as wronged and wounded; the world is always against him, it is never his fault. If only everybody knew what a nice little boy he is! When one watches this kind of pathological behavior, it becomes obvious that "the world" is nothing but the extension and projection of the patient's childhood perceptions and that this pathetic childhood situation is eternally transferred into adult experience. Whenever someone complains: "It's a cold world," I answer almost without thinking: "Your mother could not have been a very warm person. Was she?" And the perplexed response: "How did you know?" proves only that the neurotic is not only unwilling to meet his adult life as an adult, but is unable to, since he does not perceive the world in adult terms. He does not see this cold mother as a pathetic figure, herself unable to control the course of her life. He still sees her as he saw her in his childhood—strong and power-ful, cold and rejecting by conscious and deliberate design. Even if he recognizes that his own aggressive behavior covers insecurity and fear, he does not believe that the same distortion could have been operating in her case. The mother of our childhood is always above human frailty.

Basically, all neurosis, no matter what form it takes, springs from an unsolved internal conflict among the instinctual drives: the id; the conscious directing center, the ego; and the moral agency psychoanalysis calls the superego. The neurotic pattern is, initially, an attempt to escape from loneliness, to win the affection and esteem of the world by sacrificing some part of one's own needs in order to make oneself acceptable to the all-powerful and all-important parents. The conflict develops early in the child's life, and is conditioned by the family situation, the pattern into which the individual is born.

His earliest environment, with its struggles and frustrations, its rewards and punishments, is the ground on which the basic foundation is laid for all of man's later reactions to himself and to others. This is where his character is formed, the sum total of all his responses, his ways of thinking, feeling and behaving. For man is more than his inheritance through his genes, more than the unique organic structure we call constitution. These, to be sure, play an important role in each man's development. But in addition, the whole rhythm of his life, his attitudes and his beliefs is influenced by the complex mosaic of his early childhood experiences, which become the skeleton around which his future is built. Although each new experience adds something, modifying and expanding the original pattern, it is always from this matrix that the individual evaluates and anticipates the behavior of others and establishes his habitual patterns of response.

This early conditioning, with its enormous impact, begins long before the infant is able to defend himself against it. For man is not born free. He is born dependent. He is dependent on others for his very survival; his basic biological needs involve him from the moment of birth in psychological relationships. The infant is bound to others by his very helplessness; he has no choice but to accept the rules his parents lay down for him. Because these rules are directed towards molding the infant into a being acceptable to his parents and his culture, the parents must, from the very beginning, forbid and block the direct expression of many of the child's instinctual impulses. If the infant does not learn to express and satisfy himself in socially acceptable fashions, if he does not learn to tolerate a certain amount of frustration and discipline in exchange for the rewards of love and social values, he will never be able to live in peace with other people.

The basic rules and taboos of his life are initially imposed on the child from the outside, by his parents. But very soon he begins to incorporate them into himself and to experience them as originating within himself, and then they become the internal moral agency called the superego or the conscience. If in the course of his growth the child cannot modify and resolve the conflicting demands of id, ego and superego, he becomes too confused to make any reasonable adjustment. He can satisfy each only at the expense of the others, and since all are always pressing for fulfillment, he cannot achieve real satisfaction in any area of his life.

If the conflict is relatively mild, we call it a neurosis. If it affects deeper layers, psychosis. In either case, the individual feels himself unable to carry on the struggle. Everything has become too complex, too difficult to adjust to. His differing demands cannot be reconciled, and so he retreats into a safe world of his own creation, his own fantasy. He retreats, in other words, into a life of undisturbed loneliness.

If the inevitable frustrations of early childhood and the child's hostile reactions to them cannot be overcome or adjusted, it becomes impossible for him successfully to hold his personality structure together, to build the necessary internal bridge. Consequently, it becomes equally impossible to build a bridge to the outside world. Thus childhood frustration and the ensuing hate can become man's greatest enemies, the iron curtain he himself calls down against his own happiness.

It is for this reason psychoanalysts are so insistent that parents recognize their responsibility to their children from early infancy, that they do not impose burdens the child is still too young to assume. Education means teaching the child to accept necessary frustrations without resentment. This requires of the parents the utmost tact and a feeling for nuances. Rough comments and nagging, constant reproaches and punishment are in their effects as detrimental as the "overprogressive" thesis: let the child do whatever it wants.

The harmony and inner balance of the delicate triangle situation of father, mother and child is a basic condition for the child's healthy growth. Any disruption or break in any of the invisible joints spells disaster. Parents should be aware of the fact that any scene, even any tension between them to which the child is exposed is sensed and experienced by the child in a magnified manner. If the parents have to fight with one another, if they are unable to avoid scenes and mutual recriminations, then at least they should postpone them until the child is asleep or out of sight. Otherwise, they harm his very life line.

In the same way, parents must be aware that they endanger their child if they make him the battleground on which they fight out their own antagonisms and aggressions. This, too, can lead to dire results, based on the child's need to identify with his parents.

I remember a young father in his early thirties who was accused before the court of having beaten his six-year-old

son so badly that the child was seriously injured. When I
saw the father in an initial interview, I asked him why he
had done it. Didn't he love the boy? Well, he thought he
did. He could not think of any explanation for his behavior. He answered all of my questions with a stubborn
politeness, his face unmoved and wooden. Of course, he
loved his wife. He had a profession and, of course, he was
successful. Did he have friends? Oh, yes, why not? Everybody has friends. I knew he was lying, and I realized that
the only way to penetrate the mask was by a direct attack.

"Your own father must have been quite a man, eh?" I
asked casually.

"Of course he was."

"Warm and affectionate?"

"Certainly. Why not?" he responded in the same way as
before, but I thought I could detect a slight flicker in his
strained eyes. This was my chance.

"He beat you mercilessly, didn't he?" I said.

"Never."

"Why do you lie to me? I am neither your judge nor
your prosecutor. I want to help you. I am a physician. I
know that you must have suffered terribly, ordeal after
ordeal."

He swallowed hard. "Well, sometimes . . ."

"Sometimes?"

"He didn't know. He certainly didn't mean to harm me."

"But he did."

Biting his lip, he nodded.

"You loved him?"

"I hated him. I loathed him," he finally blurted out.
His face was white and he looked frightened.

"Then, if you yourself know what such suffering is like,
why do you do the same thing to your child?"

"I don't know"—his voice was tortured—"I don't know."

"Don't you realize what he is going through? Can't you understand from your own experience?"

"I don't know," he almost screamed. "Let me go, please. Can I leave now?"

"You can leave whenever you want. You are no longer a child and your father is no longer around to tell you what to do, or to beat you."

He looked straight at me for the first time. He seemed quieter now. Again I asked: "Why did you beat him?"

And again he repeated, "I don't know." His voice was softer now and he shook his head slowly from side to side. "I really don't know."

"Maybe you wanted to be like your father? Maybe you were only imitating him and reliving your own childhood, going through the same ordeal all over again, not out of vengeance but because you identified yourself with your child."

"Maybe."

"Maybe you wanted to suffer by making him suffer?"

This time he did not answer. Nor had I expected that he would. I saw him a few more times, and when I discharged him I felt that basically he had accepted what I had tried to convey to him. Accepted what? That as a child he had wanted to be punished, to be beaten, and that he had even challenged his parents in order to get this punishment, which to him meant contact with them and expiation of the heavy burden of guilt they had placed on him. And that as an adult, in his search for identification with his now-vanished childhood, he was still following the old pattern.

This desire to be hurt is called masochism, and this story shows how closely masochism is linked to sadism, each one side of the same coin. Both serve as a means of atonement for a childhood sin, either real or fancied, carried over into adult life: the guilt of masturbation, or of envy, hate and murderous resentment toward those the child is supposed to love—his parents, or others. But what was an emotional reality in childhood becomes irrational and unreal when it continues as an automatic guide for adult conduct. When man reaches maturity, he is supposed to have learned that most of his childhood behavior was a logical consequence of his parents' behavior and he is supposed to grow out of his childhood feeling of guilt and isolation.

In the complex household of the psyche these masochistic drives hide behind all kinds of disguises. The scale extends from the young girl who does not realize that she constantly defeats herself because she feels, unconsciously, that she does not deserve to succeed, to the husband who gets sexual stimulation and excitement only when he is beaten by his wife.

An intelligent and attractive young woman whom I treated several years ago was the perfect example of all those who have developed rationalization into a fine art. These are the men and women who are unmarried because "the social difficulties of our time make it impossible for anyone to meet a suitable mate," or who sit at home anxiously resentful and full of self-pity and swear that all men, or all women, are unreliable, unfaithful, and interested only in getting their own "fun." Or they go to parties only to feel more lonely than ever before and they blame everyone else for their unhappiness because they are not aware that they frighten people off with their challenging behavior and unkind remarks. In their professional lives, such people seem on the surface to do everything to please their superiors only to find themselves fired because, without being aware of it, they have made every single mistake possible.

This young woman had, after many attempts to find an adequate life for herself, finally given up altogether and retreated into empty brooding. She lived almost entirely in the past, and it was in character that she should dress in a sloppy fashion and identify herself with Greta Garbo, whose famous "I want to be alone," she seemed to be acting out melodramatically in her own life to a tragic and yet almost farcical degree. She had been unemployed for a long period, and it took many months of treatment to get her to the point of willingness to look for a job.

One day she started her therapeutic session by announcing triumphantly that she had gotten a position as a laboratory assistant. On her way to the hospital on her first day of work, however, she fell asleep in the subway and did not wake up until the train arrived at the very last station. Even though she took the next train back, she was almost an hour late in reporting to her job. The next day she got to work on time, but made up for that by breaking eight test tubes. And on the third day—she could not explain how it had happened—she added the number of the room in which she was working to the number of white blood cells she was counting for a blood test.

When she was dismissed, she was highly indignant. She could not understand why the doctor had let her go; he was unjust, unfair, unsympathetic, he would not give her a chance, he had had it in for her from the very beginning. She had tried so hard, and look what the result had been! It was certainly not her fault! She had absolutely no comprehension of the obvious fact that unconsciously she had done the exact opposite of everything she had "wanted" to do.

The case of the young man who could achieve sexual satisfaction only in a masochistic way illustrates the lengths to which the individual can go in his desperate effort to maintain some kind of communication with another person and with the world. This brilliant physicist was very insecure about his talents; often he would begin experiments in connection with the new and original ideas he developed and then drop them abruptly when they were only half-completed. Here again the mechanism of self-defeat was at work, serving his unconscious drive for self-punishment only too well.

His early history illuminates the development of his problems. His father had abandoned the family when the boy was still quite young. The child had been beaten down physically and mentally, and had been continuously exposed to the whims and cruel domination of his masculine, overbearing mother. Pushed back into his own narcissistic loneliness, frustrated and thwarted in his growth, he had no chance to express his ambivalent feelings of love and hate towards the masterful woman who ruled his life. Consequently, his masculinity was completely broken; he could maintain the love contact he needed only by compulsive repetition of the first pattern of communication he had learned: submission to a masochistic ritual. Two fictitious channels were open to him: either his wife had to beat him, or she had to wear long brown leather gloves to stimulate his otherwise impotent sex organ. This second fetish was also related to the childhood situation; his mother had worn such gloves and they became the substitute through which, in some magic way, this grown-up child could re enact and relive the childhood distortion of his blocked sex drive.

As is so often true in these cases, the marriage functioned —if we can call it functioning—as a neurotic team. The wife complemented her husband's latent homosexuality by her own masculine aggression, and he had chosen her precisely because he saw his mother in her. Their mutual neuroses fitted together perfectly, although on the surface he appeared quite masculine and she quite feminine.

The wife's extreme guilt over her own hostile impulses impelled her to present to the world a picture of reticent naïveté. She spoke softly and usually wore an embarrassed smile. But under this malleable exterior lurked a murderous unconscious hate for her husband and for men in general.

This hate was based on what psychoanalysis calls penis envy, a phenomenon the psychiatrist meets daily in his clinical experience. Penis envy is both irrational and deeply buried, and therefore it is often difficult for the layman to believe that it exists. Nevertheless, the feeling is a basic factor in neurosis in women. In men it has its counterpart in castration fear, which one finds at the root of many masculine neuroses. Both distortions begin in childhood, when boys and girls discover the anatomical differences between the sexes. The discovery is always accompanied by a great sense of shock, for the child does not realize that the girl has a sex organ; unlike the little boy's, it is not visible. To the child it seems that the boy has and the girl has not, and this knowledge produces both fear and anger. The little boy worries lest his adornment be cut off, as a punishment. He would then be reduced to the status of the girl—an incomplete male. The little girl, as a defense against her anxiety, feels that she has to get even with boys, either by destroying their penises—that is, their manhood —or by imagining that she has one herself. In childhood, the expression of these fears may be relatively direct. But if they are carried over into adult life, as a component of neurosis, their expression is indirect and symbolic; they move a great distance from the original childhood confusion in which they are rooted.

In the case described here, the childhood fantasies were experienced, maintained and acted out in several distortions. The young man's masochism was one. His wife expressed her neurosis through her work; she was a nurse, and in this profession, under the disguise of care and sacrificing love for her patients, she displayed her castrating hate by ruling and dominating them, as she ruled her husband through sadistic beatings. She, too, had suffered in childhood. Once, when he was drunk, her cold and forbidding father had raped her, and from that time on she could communicate with the world only through her irrational desire for vengeance and her monstrous anger.

To unravel this confused and complex network of anxiety, guilt and hate, and to free the sufferers from the loneliness which their marriage had only increased, was a time-consuming and difficult problem. Again and again psychiatrists and psychoanalysts are taken to task because their treatment takes so long. But psychotherapy is successful only if the patient relives his life, layer by layer, not merely in an intellectual recounting of the facts—because knowledge alone does not cure—but as an emotional experience. And this, of necessity, takes time. The childhood period of greatest strain and shock must be recaptured in all its ugly reality, so that its symbolic reliving in the present can finally be brought to an end. These periods of shock are often experienced in the "phallic" phase, when the child learns about the difference between the sexes, and earlier, during the period of toilet training.

Anyone who watches children carefully, or who dives courageously into his own early development, will discover that a decisive emotional element accompanies the act of elimination. Freud has spoken of the "anal character," and has described its characteristic behavior pattern, which includes as its main features stinginess and aggression. Such character traits are, in his view, the emotionally transformed features, that is, the symbolic representation, of an early fixation on the anal region which, for reasons related largely to parental attitudes, becomes and remains of decisive psychological importance.

If the act of elimination becomes emotionally charged for the young child because of the way in which the mother urges and supervises it, the child is likely to hold back his feces, to resist giving the expected "gift." This response is, after all, his only weapon against his mother. The biological intestinal spasticity thus created becomes the pattern for future behavior, which remains a reaction against acceding to the wishes and wills of others who play a superior role—employers, supervisors, husbands or wives. If this childhood attitude is maintained, one meets the well-known clinical picture of chronic constipation—physical and emotional—which is so often accompanied by stinginess and a generally rigid, lonely and sadistic personality, unable to love. This anal-sadistic self-enjoyment has a strong sexual component; it represents a phase of infantile sexuality, and, when it is retained, it produces all the narcissistic symptoms that keep the individual in his miserable state of loneliness.

Dorothy was a woman in her early thirties. Her brilliant intelligence had enabled her to climb far up on the professional ladder—but not far enough; she was always one step from the top. Always there was one woman above her, and Dorothy hated this superior so violently that the situation would become unbearable and she would have to quit. It was obvious that the young woman always experienced her superior as an extension of her mother. She held several degrees and had laudatory letters of recommendation from a dozen of the best-known men and women in her field, and yet she felt unhappy, nervous, depressed and extremely hostile. Her resentment was not limited to the woman who was her professional superior at any given time, but included all the men with whom she so often got entangled. Her affairs were always of short duration; she had no scruples about indulging in sexual intercourse, and was completely unaware that her unconscious aim in her "love affairs" was sadistically to deflate and castrate the man rather than to love him. Thus she chased from one adventure to the next. Each one ended in anger and she always blamed the man who "only wanted his pleasure."

In her analysis, she lay on the couch in a silent fury, her face to the wall, her back exposed to the analyst. Stubbornly she refused to talk, to give away the psychic "dirt" she was obviously holding back, as she had held back her feces when, as a child, her mother sat for hours beside her cajoling and prodding her in vain to move her bowels. During a period of long, angry, vicious aggression against the analyst, who, notwithstanding the fact that he was a man, was experienced as a mother image, this childhood scene finally was brought back into her conscious recollection. Then Dorothy suddenly remembered that her demanding, nagging, scolding and punitive mother had, time and again, pushed an enema syringe violently into her anus and had forced her to give way and let out what she wanted to hold on to. In the following hours she not only changed her body position, but it became easy to convey to her, on the basis of the now suddenly free-flowing material, that she had identified the man's attacking penis with an enema syringe, and, of course, her hate and resistance against it had made it impossible for her ever to have an orgasm and let go toward any man in a loving embrace.

So far, we have followed two roads of escape: one into partial retreat from adult reality into childhood fantasies, the other into aggression and hate as defense against thwarted love. There is a third, in which the experience of loneliness is avoided by what we call incorporation.

A man lived many years with his beloved wife. Between them was the warmth of common thoughts and ideas, experiences and feelings. Every morning when he got up, his wife's friendly face smiled at him. At night he had only to reach over to the bed beside his to caress her hair, to touch her breast. When he felt alone, she was there, taking part in his worries and joys, his successes and his failures. The couple lived together and aged together, and then suddenly came a wasting disease, which destroyed the wife's body bit by bit, dulling the sparkle in her eyes and the eternal youthfulness of her mind. Tired, emaciated, at the end unable to recognize even the husband who was a part of herself, she lay wearily in her bed until one early morning the flickering light went out.

The husband simply could not grasp the fact that she was dead. At the funeral he stood at his wife's coffin, mechanically taking the hands of relatives and friends. The organ played; he did not hear it. The minister's words were simply a buzz in his ears. Nothing registered. Something that lives cannot suddenly disappear. Nothingness cannot really be accepted, ever.

With his bridge to the world abruptly broken, the man could do only one thing to save himself from desperation and utter loneliness: he denied the tragic reality by hugging his wife's image to himself in an eternal longing. In such a state of melancholia, the outside world is kept away, all interests and libidinal bondages are withdrawn, and the afflicted retreats to an island of misty isolation, still living his earlier life in an unreal world of dreamy imagination. The dim frontier between a normal depression and a severe emotional illness vanishes, and the sufferer almost denies his very existence. From this it is only one step to a true psychosis.

The human being must be understood in his totality, for he functions as an entity. Dubois Reymond's once famous statement about the psycho-physical parallelism, *"Ignoramus, ignorabimus,"* "We do not know, we will never know," no longer describes the facts. For today medical science has a new understanding of psychosomatic interdependence, and this understanding yields daily results in the general treatment of diseases.

Anyone who has ever been ill knows that he feels and behaves differently when he is lying on his sickbed and on the days when he feels well and healthy. Not only his mood, but his whole character seems to undergo a change. When he is ill, he is likely to be irritated, egotistic, oversensitive, easily offended, impatient and unjust. His whole approach and attitude in relation both to himself and to the world shrinks from wide interest to petty, selfish narcissism.

What is more difficult to see—and yet is just as true—is the reverse pattern: man's emotions can affect his physical health, his unconscious conflicts can be dramatized through his body.

Some persons often get into accidents. They are called "accident prone." Although these men and women do not have any conscious wish to be hurt, certain facts emerge when they are treated with the methods of deep psychology. Their accident proneness is only a single symptom of many; they have an unconscious desire to punish themselves. These deeply hidden masochistic drives become particulary significant in relation to the "flight into disease." For although illness is usually painful, uncomfortable and distressing, it can offer advantages that compensate for its discomfort and displeasure. What are the motives that lie behind this paradoxical and destructive flight into disease?

Evelyn's father had died when she was still a young child. The girl was brought up by her mother, a business woman who worked long hours to provide for herself and her daughter. Since the mother spent most of the day away from home, she left her little girl in the care of an old aunt, who was preoccupied with her own worries and showed little affection for the lonely and love-starved child. Consequently, the girl developed strong unconscious feelings of inadequacy and unworthiness. It seemed to her that her mother had deserted her. She could not understand that the older woman *had* to work, that, indeed, her work was in some degree her conscious expression of love for her child. The daughter saw herself as unloveable and was filled with resentment against both her mother and her aunt. She refused to help in the small household, and spent her days reading, burying herself in a world of fantasy. Occasionally she would write poetry, which was full of her childish sense of devastation and tragedy. The first poems she submitted for publication were rejected as dilettante. To add to her hurt and disappointment at this rebuff, her

mother accidentally found the girl's clumsy efforts at literary achievement and, without realizing the harm she was
doing her child, poked fun at the "useless and purposeless" work, at the "meaningless phrases," the "tormented
rhythm."

Shortly after this, the child fell ill. She began to cough,
her tonsils were swollen and she ran a slight temperature.
The doctor diagnosed a mild bronchitis and advised the
mother to stay home and nurse her daughter. The child's
stay in bed thus became a dearly desired honeymoon; at
last she had her mother to herself, she had attention and
affectionate concern. No wonder, then, that her illness
dragged on long beyond the normal term. The doctor was
puzzled, and even began to doubt his initial diagnosis. He
did not understand that the disease had become an unconscious instrument for the child, through which she
brought her mother closer to her and at the same time
gratified her childish hate and aggression by keeping her
mother away from her job.

Eventually, of course, the child regained her health. But
from that time on she became "sickly," and developed one
illness after another, each of which demanded her mother's
attention and care. This pattern continued even after the
child had grown up, even after her mother had died. When
she married, it became her means of getting her husband's
attention and affection whenever she felt lonely and neglected.

How exactly do emotions become converted into physical symptoms? Everyone has experienced the sweaty palms
and pounding heart of an anxiety attack. Many great artists have diarrhoea before they appear in public. Every
woman knows how closely her menstrual period is related

to her emotional state; it may be withheld and delayed because of the fear of pregnancy, it may be painful during periods of general emotional stress.

Medical men and psychiatrists have been for many years carrying on a broad research investigation to establish the relationship between personality make-up and specific diseases; to discover the tuberculosis type, the rheumatism type, the heart type, etc., and in some hospitals the percentage of cures has been markedly increased since psychiatrists have begun to work in each department, dermatological, respiratory, cardiac, gastro-intestinal, etc. The most striking findings have been in this last category, in relation to the origin and development of gastric ulcers and ulcerative colitis. In all these cases the investigators have been able to establish the operation of two main features: an overdependence on the mother and a violent fight against her, a dramatic and unresolved conflict between aggression and loneliness. The psychogenic factor in these diseases is so strong that their treatment has essentially shifted into the psychiatrist's office.

Asthma is another disease in which the psychogenic component is acknowledged to be the main operating lever, throwing a specific chemical pathology into operation. An overwhelming accumulation of clinical material, describing hundreds of thorough investigations into the psychodynamics of asthmatics, has shown a surprising similarity in personality make-up in all these cases. In most of them, the mother failed the child in early infancy. She may have been hostile and rejecting, she may have died early, she may have given the child into the care of others. Whatever the reason, the child lacked the things it needed to defend itself against insecurity and loneliness: milk, time, care and affection. The tormenting asthma attack is merely the bodily expression of a feeling of suffocation, the fearful, desperate and anxious outcry of the lonely child for its mother.

This fight against loneliness, against one's own aggression and sense of guilt, can take many physical forms. The story of a young Italian woman whose only symptom was a sudden outbreak of eczema on the face is an interesting example. This woman had been orphaned early and had been pushed around from one foster home to another. Although she searched frantically for love, she was never able to find acceptance or affection from the succession of grumpy, cold foster mothers into whose homes she was brought. She was never allowed to be a child, playful, loved and fondled. She was always unwanted and paid for, and in every home in which she was placed she had to earn her keep by helping with the cleaning or the cooking or by watching over the other children. She was screamed at and pushed around until finally she could stand it no longer and she ran away. Picked up by the police, she was brought back to her current foster mother, and from then on she was treated even more harshly. Again she ran away, and this time she escaped discovery. She went to a distant town and got herself a job in a factory, which at least enabled her to provide for herself and to be independent.

On the job she met a man who took her, brutally and coldly. The woman found herself pregnant and forced him to marry her. She had one child and after a year another, but never did she feel the satisfaction of love, the warmth of belonging or the reassurance of security. She felt only a gnawing hate of her husband, her children, and the whole world, which owed her something it refused to give. She knew she had been cheated. Every other night she had to submit her body to the brutal biology of her husband's desire, and each time she experienced her sexual relationship with him as destruction and murder. She felt as though she was being forced into something that she hated.

One day, on one of the rare occasions when her husband took her to a party, she met a handsome man who said pleasant things to her, admired her pretty face and stroked her jet-black hair caressingly. She felt a tingling sensation all over her face and body, and when the young man hinted that he was leaving the next day for Florida and would like to have her with him, she decided to join him a few days later. But after she made the decision, her conscience became extremely demanding. Was it right for her to leave her husband and her children alone for a week or more? Was it right to sneak off to a rendezvous with a man she did not really know? When she finally decided to go through with the plan, her face suddenly began to swell and an ugly eczema appeared all over the distorted surface.

"I'm ugly," she cried. "Can you understand that? How can he love me looking this way? Should I still go? Please tell me what to do!"

"It's not up to me to tell you what to do," I said. "I am not your father, and you have to live and act on your own responsibility. But in case you do decide to leave, please come here and we'll talk about it again."

She was not very happy with that answer; she wanted to use me as her conscience, and I had failed her. It was with some defiance that she left. I had a pretty good idea of what would happen, and I was not surprised when she returned, a week later. This time her face was even more swollen, and on it were bloodstained scratches she evidently had produced herself.

"See how I look?" she said accusingly.

"Yes," I answered, "I see."

"You know what happened?"

"You went to Florida, I guess."

"Only half the way," she responded with a bitter smile. I waited.

"Want to know what happened?" A vulgar expression, which I had never seen before, appeared on her face. "I slept with another man. On the train. I didn't know him at all. He gave me a lot to drink. I don't remember much of what happened. It was in his compartment. When I woke up the next morning . . ."

". . . you looked as you do now."

Suddenly she began to cry, sobbing helplessly and without restraint, like a child.

"And now you have come back to your husband and your children and to me," I said.

She nodded, blowing her red and swollen nose noisily.

In the following hours I let her work through the defiant hate which had been nothing but a protection against her lonely and hopeless craving for love. And she began to understand the struggle between the old, powerful sexual drives and her forbidding moral censorship, a battle that had ended with the dramatic self-punishment on her skin. After this, the eczema disappeared in a few days.

This psychosomatic traffic runs two ways: not only from the emotions, through the glandular switchboard to the body tissues, but the other way as well. All those who have worked in rehabilitation centers, with men crippled by war or by accidents in civilian life, and all those who are related to such afflicted persons can testify to the extent to which a partial disability of function or a deforming scar can set off an emotional problem. In addition to the extreme depression that would be expected as a result of

such realistic deprivations and injuries, pathological reactions often occur which go far beyond the scope of
passing moods and affect the whole personality, shaking its
defensive foundations to the very core. Each individual's
specific personality and character condition his responses
and reactions to the traumatic situation; in general, however, the physical disability acts as a trigger, reopening all
the old psychic wounds, tearing asunder all the psychic
defenses. The parapets built with so much painful care
through a lifetime crumble away, and the poor, naked ego
lapses back into its old state of freezing loneliness.

Ben was one of those who had managed to "forget" his
damaging childhood . . . although never completely. At
the age of six he had been stricken by a polio infection
which had temporarily affected the muscles of his right leg.
In about two years the paralyzing effect subsided and the
only reminder of his illness was a barely perceptible limp.
But during that two years the sensitive child had been exposed to parental attitudes and behavior that left a deep
scar on his later character. His mother and father had carried the bewildered little boy from one doctor to the next.
Anxious and oversolicitous, they exposed him for long
months to a constant barrage of electric treatments, massages, hot baths and all sorts of medication. This hectic,
neurotic, almost panicky overactivity in itself left the child
with the feeling that he was inadequate, unfit for life and
helpless. His low self-esteem was depressed even further
by his mother, who called him a cripple who was ruining
her life. To this irresponsible woman, a child could only
be a kind of adornment for her own mediocrity. And since
his disease had turned her son into a liability rather than
an asset to be bragged about, she hated him; all her display
of extravagant concern was actually only a flimsy cover, an

attempt to compensate for her guilt. She felt disappointed, cheated by the gods, she was full of animosity and bitterness, which she communicated to her son in everything she did. This "bad mother" was herself a pathetic figure, the product of a difficult childhood, who destroyed herself as well as her son.

Although Ben's muscular paralysis disappeared, the paralyzing experience remained and his entire character development was a reaction to it. As a child he was anxious, prone to temper tantrums, and he wet his bed—all expressions both of his lonely hate for his mother and his vengeful and desperate struggle for her love. After a year these symptoms disappeared, and now Ben began to read compulsively through half the night and to work tenaciously at school until he was the best in his class.

His father, ambitious and driving himself, a successful, self-made builder whose concern employed dozens of workers, became Ben's ideal. Relentlessly, the boy threw all his energies into study and work; he had to become at least as big as father; bigger, if possible. He had to compensate for his bodily injury although by now he had forgotten about it and only the reaction to it remained. Eventually he became the successful owner of an art gallery; his "cultural" occupation seemed to link him with a world of spiritual values, a world in which neither his father nor his mother could successfully compete with him.

Everything went well, at least on the surface, until the day of Pearl Harbor. Again Ben had to prove himself and although the Army doctor was reluctant to accept him because of his slight limp, he was commissioned a second lieutenant. He rose rapidly to the rank of captain and received the highest insignia for extraordinary bravery. He never spared himself, but dared the most dangerous situa-

tions to prove to himself and to the world—his parents—
that he was not incompetent or unworthy.

One day, when again he had exposed himself unspar-
ingly to enemy fire, a bomb exploded right beside him.
The young lieutenant who had been his devoted and ad-
miring friend and several soldiers whom he commanded
were torn to pieces. Ben himself was seriously wounded
and two fingers of his left hand had to be amputated. He
received a medical discharge, and when he came out of the
hospital, honored by the Purple Heart and a special cita-
tion, he felt limp and dazed. He withdrew from all his
friends and social contacts; he refused to go to his office
and resume control of his business, and he retreated into
a stupor-like loneliness, which he could neither force himself out of nor master. He had experienced the second
injury as a repetition of the childhood trauma. His war
wounds revived all the misery and loneliness of the suffering child and seemed to prove that all his struggle to compensate for his disability, to achieve success, had been for
nothing. He was but an unloved, forlorn and crippled
child.

The self-punishing retaliation and irrational feeling of
vengeance in the cases so far discussed are operative in
practically every neurotic. They represented an escape
reaction from a general fear of being hurt in adult life as
in childhood. It is easy then to understand why such
bruised and lonely victims should search for a way out of
their loneliness by substituting animal pets for the human
beings whom they dread and fear. A pet is not frightening. It gives its master affection and unbroken love and it
receives affection without making any demands. In addition, a pet provides its owner with the chance to feel important, making it unnecessary for him to prove himself.

The pet does not expose him to the ugly strain of constant criticism.

This warm, hairy dog with its swimming golden eyes will come to you whenever you call it, whenever you need it. It will follow you and obey you and love you, whatever you do and whoever you are. Whether you beat it or caress it, feed it with all kinds of delicacies or leave it half-starved, it will cry when you leave and bark and wag its tail and behave with frantic joy when you return. It will always look up to you with unstinting admiration and affection, it will wait for you faithfully, and will try to please you by displaying all the ridiculous little tricks you have taught it. It will never hurt you, never disappoint you. "In the eyes of my dog lies all my happiness," a European poet once wrote.

What causes these animals to behave as they do? We do not know. Some people have tried to explain their all encompassing affection and devotion by narrowing them down to a primitive gratitude towards anyone who feeds them or gives them a dry, warm place in which to lie down. Perhaps this explanation is correct. But even if it is, even if gratitude is the simple and only motivation for all the dog's passionate affection, it does not minimize its value or the blessed miracle of its intensity. Thus, it is not surprising that those who are starved for love, for the simple, uncomplicated display of affectionate devotion, who are tired from the disappointments, the pains and the hurts of their daily struggles with other human beings, should give all their warmth to their pets. It is much more peaceful and rewarding to give up the fight and to find a companion which will give its love unreservedly and whose affection can be reciprocated without fear of being suddenly stabbed in the heart.

Of course, there are nuances. There is the childless, lonely, middle-aged woman who strokes and spoils her small, pudgy poodle. There is the famous judge who ignores all his party guests to sit down on the floor and play with his cocker spaniel. Sometimes the motive is not love: hate, too, can become a means of escape from loneliness. There is the svelte, well-tailored, broad-shouldered young woman who walks along the street with hard, masculine steps, a cigarette in her mouth and a huge, nervous Irish setter pulling and tearing her along. Here the beautiful red animal, whose color matches perfectly the tinted red hair of its owner, serves as an adornment, showing off the girl's masculine drive for domination and power. The cruel beatings she probably administers to the animal are substitutes for the beatings she would like to give all men—whom she thoroughly despises.

But this is the exception. The rule is to give great, unrestrained tenderness to a creature that needs you, that represents not the feared adult, but the helpless child. Often it is deeply touching to see the degree to which a dog's owner identifies with the little creature, displaying towards it all the affection which he himself wanted so desperately and never received.

It is not surprising, then, that the death of an animal should often bring a consuming grief to its owner. There are cases in which dogs have refused to leave the dead bodies of their masters and have sat motionless for days, crying and refusing to take any food. But the story can be told in reverse, too: an eminent architect refused to eat, retreated from all his social engagements and found himself unable to go on with his professional life for weeks after his dog had been killed by a carelessly driven automobile.

Near Paris is a cemetery reserved for animals. Up the

Seine, in the dreary suburb of Asnières, in the middle of the river, lies a tiny island: Île des Ravageurs. Once this island was the site of duels of honor: today it holds the animal cemetery, in which repose an elephant and a tiger that died in captivity while displaying their domesticated wildness in a circus. A few canaries rest here, too, and a few cats. And, of course, dogs.

The graves are little mounds. Most are topped by simple signs, made of wood or metal, on which are inscribed the names of the dead animals. Others are more ornate, adorned with pictures and verses, endearing little words full of an overpowering grief and tenderness. The cemetery is full now, and not even the stiff body of a canary could find a resting place between the small grave mounds. In the spring, when the river is swollen, the graves near the embankment are flooded by the blue-gray water, and when it recedes, it leaves a greenish mud around them, choked with the debris of leaves and particles that the great stomach of the city has disgorged.

This morning it had rained. The roads were soft and wet and a silvery blue mist hung lifeless between the naked branches of the trees. A young Parisian woman in her thirties, wearing a simple blue silk frock of exquisite style, walked into the cemetery. Without hesitation, she went to a grave she knew, to which she must have gone before, probably innumerable times. Bending down, she took away the withered flowers and laid in their place a bouquet of red carnations. Then she knelt down. She did not bother to arrange her costly dress, nor did she seem to care whether her expensive shoes were spoiled by the soft mud. Cautiously she put down a small container of gold fluid she had brought with her and, with a fine brush, began to fill in the engraved letters on the tombstone. Never have I seen an expression of such tender grace and despairing attention as in this gesture of a woman who had come all the way from her luxurious life to this dingy spot because she could not forget the jumping joy of her faithful companion.

Is this sentimental? Neurotic? Perhaps both. And still one cannot pass coldly over a scene that seems like a trembling reflection of the gods' saddest smile.

CHAPTER FIVE

❖

Road Map Extension

THE HUMAN RACE, itself merely a quantitative extension of the family, has been forced, gradually and painfully, to acknowledge that no community, no society, can
exist without rules and regulations. The child, sitting in
the lonely center of his world, has to learn step by step that
he is not alone, that he can only find freedom in the acceptance of social responsibility. He learns this through the
process of education. And education necessarily involves
frustration: frustration in acting out one's own instinctual
drives, frustration that must ultimately be accepted without resentment.

If it is not accepted, if the rights and privileges of others
—both in the family and in the broader world—are neglected, and the individual concerns himself only with his
own wishes, he will remain for his whole life in a state of
loneliness, out of which he creates a world of misery and
unreality. Thus the establishment and acceptance of rules,
although often hard to take, helps man to conquer loneliness by helping him to relate successfully to the world outside himself.

A good-looking Canadian girl of twenty-three had
opened the veins in her wrist in a suicide attempt. She was
the daughter of what one might call millionaire com-
munists; her father had come from a poor background and

suffered such severe guilt because he had piled up an enormous fortune in a comparatively short time, that he felt compelled to put on a show of extreme social, political and cultural tolerance. The mother accepted the father's position with all its implications, and young Maude grew up in an atmosphere in which everything was allowed and nothing forbidden or even severely criticized.

One morning it happened that Maude decided to have her breakfast under the table.

"Darling," her mother began to plead cautiously when on entering the room, she saw dishes, bread, milk, sugar, butter and eggs on the floor, "don't you think it would be better and more comfortable . . ."

"No Mother, I don't," the child interrupted, her mouth full of thickly buttered toast. "It's fun. I like it here. You can't understand that. And you always try to spoil my fun." She wiped her fingers, sticky with strawberry jam, on the light gray carpet.

"I certainly don't want to disturb your fun, honey, and I understand perfectly that it must be really grand to play Indian under the table. But . . ."

"Then why don't you join me? Let's all have breakfast here. It's clean fun."

When the father arrived, the latest political and art periodicals under his arm, the mother pointed with a helpless gesture at their offspring.

"Please, you try," she whispered, a bit tense.

"What are you doing down there, sweetheart?" the father opened the attack in his most honeyed voice.

"Come down here and you'll see . . ."

"But don't you see . . ."

"You are really awful bores, both of you. And please stop arguing, Daddy. You're just old-fashioned. If Mommy insists on standing around up there and nagging me, you just come down here without her and we'll have a good time, I promise."

"Your mother only wants the best for you, sweetie."

"Yes, yes, I know. Oh, God! Are you coming down here or aren't you?"

"O.K."

And so it happened that on this morning the whole family had "fun" breakfasting under the table; this day and the following day and whenever it struck Maude's fancy.

The parents felt that this was progressive education. Never tell the child what to do. No inhibitions, no narrow rules. Let the child do as it wants; our youngsters shall be free, strong and healthy, happy citizens one day of a truly democratic world!

Young Maude somehow managed to pass her school examinations although she went to classes only when she felt like it. It was all very boring and the teachers were all "great dopes." When she entered college, in New York, she did not know what subjects to study. All were good or bad alike. She started with languages, switched to philosophy, and then, of course, changed to psychology. But the courses, she felt, were dull. So she switched again—to chemistry, then medicine and finally, to journalism. Then she gave up "the whole nonsense," because she decided that she did not need "academic guidance."

The thing to do, she was now convinced, was to act out one's emotions. She started to do this by taking violin lessons. Then she began to paint and sculpt. But it was all nothing—all no good. For two months she spent her waking hours writing a novel at a huge desk she had proudly purchased for three hundred dollars in an antique shop. When she finished that, she wrote three short stories, two plays and a film scenario. She offered her creations to book publishers, magazine editors and theatrical agents and they were all returned. She was furious. Nobody understood her. They were all nincompoops and ignoramuses. Who cares?

Anyway, the whole experiment had been a mistake. She threw out the desk and her typewriter (they took up too much space) and devoted herself to "living," which meant sex. She spent her evenings at dances, parties and nightclubs. She went to bed—after short acquaintance—with nearly every man she met, and changed her partner nearly every week. When I saw her, she had had two abortions and had been treated for venereal disease. Finally, what else can one do but open one's veins and cut one's wrists so that the boring, useless and lonely life can stream away from the broken and diseased mind and body?

What to do with her? How to treat her? If I had put her on the couch and asked her to tell me whatever came into her mind in order to make conscious what had been repressed into the unconscious by the moral censorship of her superego, I would only have repeated the same mistake her well-meaning yet short-sighted parents had committed. Therefore, I took just the opposite tack. I began by discouraging her from doing certain things, each time explaining the reason for the taboo. I suggested that for the time being she should stay away from sex, which had obviously given her no gratification and had been only an expression of her aggression against men. I urged her to get a job—even a menial one—and to try to live within the income that job provided.

Slowly Maude built up a scale of values that had not previously existed. It was of course not without great resistance and violent outbursts that she began to grasp the fact that if everything is permitted, nothing is of value. It was equally difficult for her to realize that it does not limit the boundaries and joys of one's own life to put voluntary restrictions on one's impulses out of consideration for the wishes and feelings of others, but that, on the contrary, such limitations actually enrich the individual and lead away from narcissistic loneliness. It was a hard and trying school for this spoiled child, and more than once she threatened to run away from the painful treatment. But finally, she herself chose voluntarily to channel her instinctual drives into constructive activities. And I noticed with increasing joy that day by day the deep lines of contemptuous self-pity, boredom and depression on her face diminished, and a new sparkle of life grew in her heretofore dead eyes. Now, a few years later, Maude is happily married and has a baby she loves. Finally her life contains all the satisfactions and enjoyment for which she had earlier searched in vain.

Rules, laws, limitations and frustrations are a necessity for man's existence; the educational process itself, with its training in partial self-denial, demonstrates with painful clarity that life cannot be directed only towards pleasure. The child rebels against all these necessary frustrations almost from the moment of his birth, and if the educational process fails in some way, this rebellion grows into hostility—initially directed against the frustrating parents and eventually against the whole world, so that the individual finds himself trapped by his own anger and hate. Hostility, if unchecked, can grow into general anti-social behavior and finally blossom in crime. Thus we might say that in the case of the criminal we are dealing with a paradoxical situation. He has been rejected from the beginning, by his father or mother or both, in his search for love. Thrown back into himself and his own loneliness, his compulsive criminal drives become the substitute link and ultimately his only link to a hostile world. Crime becomes his means of communication. This is the reason for the constant relapse of the great majority of criminals, which no prison, no penalty, seems to deter. It is the reason, too, for the comparatively bad results psychiatrists have observed in their psychotherapeutic attempts with these lonely people.

Almost invariably, when the psychiatrist goes into the history of such cases, he meets the tragic account, recited bitterly and with resentment, of a broken home; or a rude drinking father; or violent scenes between husband and wife; or beatings and screams and an atmosphere of fright and bewilderment from which there was only one way out: escape into hate and isolation. The loneliness and self-seclusion of every criminal is painfully evident in his behavior. He hardly ever responds to kindness or affectionate friendliness; he is irritated, rather than helped, by it. His one way out is his hate, which itself brings an unconscious craving for punishment. The criminal's complex reactions have their parallel in the behavior of unhappy children; every criminal act is a challenge; after it is committed, the punishment is usually accepted with a startling serenity.

Only an hour ago, Tim, a man in his thirties, reported a dream. "There was a gathering of juvenile complainers," he remembered, "presided over by President Eisenhower. One of the kids was a bit older. He was dressed in black and wore a hat, which he refused to take off, even though he was urged to do so, as an act of reverence, by several people. The atmosphere was like one of the President's press conferences, and the boy in black felt great pity for Eisenhower, who looked sick."

In discussing this dream, Tim was quick to understand that the rebellious youth must have been the dreamer himself; that Eisenhower was the analyst, an image of his father, and that his act of defiance was coupled with sorrow and pity. But the most significant factor, which he did not immediately grasp, was that he still considered himself a "juvenile," a spokesman for all the other "complainers." In other words, he still clings to his ambivalent childhood feelings towards his father, and this is evident in the fact that he transfers them into his adult social, political and emotional life.

Timmy's aggressions and violence overflow into every field of human relations, and are especially evident in his attitude towards women. He has constantly to conquer them to prove himself; he chases from one to the next, never loving, never getting any real joy out of his conquests. He has to beat women down and attack them as he has to beat down all the competition he meets, in his job, in his social life, because his only way of making contact with others is through his hate. Timmy is, then, a potential criminal, who might easily transfer to any authority his murderous defiance of the laws and rules his father laid down in his childhood. His refusal to recognize custom and social regulations, as demonstrated in his dream by his refusal to take off his hat, is merely the little boy's vengeance for not being loved. Timmy identifies society and the whole world with his father, whose "crime" was that he himself did not recognize his son's craving for love.

Timmy's mother had been a short-tempered woman who was early forced into a loveless marriage; she was irritated most of the time and her son's life was a round of "shut up," and "you know everything, don't you?" These repeated, impatient, angry assaults usually ended with her screaming accusation: "You're full of egotism." To which the boy, in desperate hurt, would respond with the enlightening remark: "That's all I have."

This mother and father did not see the frenzied struggle of their child for love. They did not understand that their child's "egotism" was the consequence of their own emotional coldness; it was all he had because he had to give up the battle for love as lost. He had to retreat into a loneliness from which there was only one way out: hate and a murderous defiance that might easily lead him onto the road of crime.

The question remains, of course, why certain persons limit their aggressive, hostile and murderous drives to mere fantasies and dreams, while others act them out. For the aggressive fantasies which have their origins in childhood frustrations remain a part of the life of normal persons who show no overt criminal behavior. These fantasies find expression in mankind's fascination and preoccupation with murder and crime. People enjoy mystery stories and horror movies because they identify with them.

The criminal, however, by the very fact that he acts out his impulses and uses his crimes as a link to the "hostile" world, cannot be considered normal. Yet he need not be psychotic. Scientists continue to search for the reasons for criminality and the development of the criminal character. Some have postulated special constitutional and hereditary bodily factors. Others have looked for the signs and stigmata of degenerative processes. In my opinion, none of these suggestions is completely convincing. For in every case of criminal behavior, whether the criminal is psychotic or not, I have found only one common factor: the child's normal love relationship with his parents was blocked and frustrated.

A mild-mannered college teacher, whose gentle and persuasive manner had made his lectures the most popular at the university, was loved and admired by everyone who knew him. He was in great demand as a public speaker and was a leader in the community. Nobody suspected that this amiable young man had dreams in which he cut off his father's head and flung it into the toilet bowl.

One day, after he had been in treatment for a short time, he got up from the couch and silently, without any display of emotion, emptied his bowels on my carpet. The next day came another act of defiance: he opened the fly of his trousers and began to play quietly with his genital. He dared to act out his dreams, and I watched him cautiously from then on; one day he might start a direct murderous attack against me. This was a potential criminal and, of course, a schizophrenic.

There was not much difference between him and the middle-aged woman who one day decided to throw the pillow on my couch out of the window. When I grabbed her arm—because I liked my pillow—she took this as a signal to shift her attack against me. She was muscular and strong, and almost succeeded in her endeavor. She ripped my shirt open from top to bottom and nearly had me out the window when I finally broke free and reached the telephone. The police arrived after an agony of waiting, and the patrol car took her to a hospital, from which she was committed to a state asylum. About a year later, while she was still a patient there, she wrote me a warm and friendly postcard expressing her affection and love. She could not grasp the fact that both in her attack and her affectionate protestations she was acting out her ambivalent feelings toward her dead father, which she had projected onto me.

Another facet of crime must be understood—the psychology of the thief which, although very different on the surface from attack and assault, has pretty much the same motivations.

If a little boy is hungry and his mother does not have the money with which to buy him bread, it would not be surprising if he stole a loaf from the bakery counter. The theft can be easily understood; it indicates both the boy's hunger and the weakness of his moral ramparts, which are not strong enough to withstand the overwhelming drive of self-preservation. Much the same dynamics operate in the case in which a mother gives her child a few pennies to buy a loaf of bread and he treats himself to some tempting bubble gum instead. Even if he later tells her tearfully that he lost the money, one would probably smile sympathetically at the child's "weakness" and forget all about it.

A man crossing the high bridge over the swollen river that ran through one of Europe's beautiful university towns noticed a girl of about nine being carried rapidly down the stream. He jumped in and succeeded in pulling her to the bank by her long flowing hair. But he was too late. She was dead. He tried to revive her, pressing rhythmically on her sides; as he did this, he noticed a brown fluid streaming from her nose and from the corner of her white lips. A few hours later the hysterical mother reported that she had given the child some money to buy meat and vegetables for supper, but, as she had discovered by checking with the grocery store when her child did not return home, the girl had asked instead for half a pound of chocolate and had eaten it all. Then, in a panic of anticipated punishment, she had jumped into the water.

This pathetic little crime and self-punishment shows how brutal and destructive can be the effect of a conscience that represents the incorporation of a cold and forbidding mother. In this case, the child had to look for her pitiful pleasures secretly, she could not get the desired "sweets" from her strict mother.

This symbolism in even sharper form dominates and somehow explains the puzzling structure of the criminal acts called kleptomania. In contradistinction to the true thief, the kleptomaniac has neither any realistic need for what he takes, nor can he expect any gain from it. The nineteen-year-old college girl, on whose behalf I was asked to testify in court, had all the material advantages. Her closet was filled with exquisite clothing of all kinds, suits and dresses and shoes of all styles and colors. In her dresser lay row on row of sheer stockings, nightgowns and underclothes. She had a small green leather box filled with jewelry, including a small gold pin and a ring with three little diamonds, a gift from her sorority. She seemed to have everything, with one exception—the love of her mother.

Her parents had been divorced when Jeanne was still very young, and the child hardly remembered her father. She and her mother lived in a huge apartment that was furnished in cold splendor and false elegance. But neither the oversized rooms of the apartment nor the silent and dead glory of two Cadillacs could fill the feeling of emptiness Jeanne tried to cover up under a mask of sociability and charm. Behind the façade of forced gaiety and restless party glamor bled a wound of empty loneliness. Jeanne's admired, shyly desired and hated mother had utterly neglected her. The daughter's efforts to achieve social success, her masquerade as a gay princess were simply imitations of her mother's behavior, with the difference that the mother actually enjoyed her irresponsibility, while it made her daughter ill.

One day when she had nothing better to do, Jeanne went to a department store at which her mother had a charge account. She wandered aimlessly around, from one section to another, from one counter to another, until she playfully grabbed three handkerchiefs and, following an irresistible impulse, let them disappear into her handbag. This pathetic incident was watched by the store detective, who promised to let her go if she signed a statement that she would never come back into the store. She obligingly signed it—and promptly came back the next day. Again she wandered around and again she was watched by the attentive detective. This time she picked up two pairs of stockings and, as she dropped them into her bag, she was apprehended.

A trial followed. Unfortunately, the judge was one of those calcified old gentlemen for whom the psychiatric expert was, in his words, "the same as a magician, a palm reader or a quack." He refused to permit me to testify and disposed the case angrily, levying a fine of $100 against the girl and threatening her with a prison sentence if her "crime" was repeated. Had he given a moment's thought to the fact that there was no overt motivation at all in this case, that Jeanne had ample money with which to purchase both the handkerchiefs and the stockings whenever or wherever she wanted to, he would have realized that he was not dealing with a common criminal, but with a sick young woman.

What was the sickness? What were the real motives for her strange behavior? What lay behind the sudden and overwhelming impulse to take something she did not need? It is not difficult to understand that the handkerchiefs and the stockings were merely symbols, and that what Jeanne really stole was her mother's affection, which had been so tragically withheld from her, and which she had to claim at whatever cost.

In addition to the irrational symbolism of kleptomania the pathological flight from loneliness can take many forms. The most truly tragic of these is psychosis, in which the sealing-off process, the denial of the outside world, becomes almost complete. Once I was called upon to treat a young photographer who confused his approach to life with his approach to his profession. He somehow only "photographed" the world around him and consequently complained about his feeling of loneliness. He stood alone in its center, with his photographic brain registering all the lines, forms and colors with great artistic sensitivity, yet unable to identify anything around him as actual and real, like he, himself.

Modern psychiatrists and analysts no longer think of the differences between neurosis and psychosis in the same rigid way they did only five years ago. Their experience has shown that the frontiers and transitions from one into the other are much more fluid and sliding than it was previously thought and, diagnostically, they are much more interested in the psychodynamics of the specific patient than in the superficial grouping of symptoms. However, more and more it becomes clear that psychosis, no less than many "physical" diseases, is a psychosomatic problem. Psychiatrists are now inclined to think that in the cases of actual psychosis there is a very deep disturbance of constitutional factors and bodily functions, especially of glands, hormones and metabolism, and that these disturbances make the individual prone to fall into mental disease if he is confronted with a difficult social situation.

Until a few years ago, the only techniques for dealing with the psychoses were the purely physical methods: electric and insulin shock, and psychosurgery, such as lobotomy. In recent years has come the development of the biochemical compounds, such as the tranquillizers. Today, in dealing with these cases psychiatry has begun to try to rebuild the broken bridge by the slow process of psychotherapy, individually or in groups. Though the old methods have by no means been abandoned, it is obvious that nobody is actually cured by shock treatment alone. The shock serves merely as a kind of preparatory heavy artillery attack to level down and break through the patient's formidable psychological defenses. It is only after the brutal push and removal of the ego from its retreat and isolation that the patient and doctor can work through the complexity of causes to the root of the problem, so that ultimately cure can be effected. If this is not done, the patient is most likely to relapse into his former withdrawal and his state of disorganized retreat from reality after a short period of improvement and pseudo cure.

What does psychosis look like? What are the impressions one gets when entering one of the wards in a mental institution? The common denominator in all the strange, often frightening and seemingly incomprehensible behavior one sees is the patient's tight seclusion from a reality that has been too painful to bear. The psychotic lives in a substitute world, a world of his own creation. He may enjoy it in pleasant fantasies and dreams of grandeur, or it may have been emptied and brushed clean of any kind of emotional response at all. The patient may be catatonic or violent, but in either case, what one observes in psychosis is a self-imposed loneliness, into which the individual has retreated because the experiences of reality, especially and most usually in his childhood, have been too much to endure.

Several years ago I received a telephone call from a friend, a famous musician, who had married a woman many years younger than himself.

"Something is the matter with Ellen." He sounded panic-struck. "She doesn't know what day it is. She doesn't even recognize me. You've got to come over."

I hurried to his home as quickly as I could, and when I arrived found the young woman slumped in a chair.

"Hello, Ellen," I said. "I haven't seen you for at least two weeks."

She looked at me blankly.

"Of course, you know who I am, don't you?"

"No," she replied tonelessly.

"You know *him*, though, don't you?" I pointed to her husband. But again came the same expressionless "no."

Now her husband became hysterical: "But monkey . . . monkletty."

There was no response.

I realized that something drastic had to be done, and quickly. I took her in my car to a sanitarium, where she was knocked into unconsciousness by an electric shock treatment. She woke up bewildered, looking around herself like someone who has overslept.

"Where am I? Where is my husband? What am I doing here?" she asked wonderingly.

"You know who I am?" I tested her.

"But of course, silly. What's this all about?"

She seemed perfectly normal and I had difficulty in persuading her and her husband that she should stay at the sanitarium at least a few days, to rest.

That afternoon the nurse phoned me.

"You'd better come right back, Doctor. She doesn't recognize anyone."

It was only six hours since I had left her, and now she was back in her original state of stubborn refusal, answering every question put to her with a monotonous "I don't know."

At once, I gave her a second shock, increasing both the duration and the intensity of the electric current. Again after she recovered consciousness she showed the same reaction: she wondered where she was and seemed completely normal.

This time I insisted on keeping her for two weeks and gave her six more shocks.

"You have cured her!" her husband thanked me profusely.

"Unfortunately, I haven't," I said. "This is only the beginning. She'll need analytic treatment now if she is to find out what causes this and if this situation is to be prevented from happening all over again."

"She seems fine to me, but . . ."

Although she was obviously reluctant, Ellen came for intense psychoanalytic treatment for three months. Gradually, she got some insight into the unconscious drives, impulses and motivations behind her behavior.

She had been an only child. Her mother had died when

Ellen was sixteen, and the child had in a sense taken over the mother's role. The father, tall, handsome and very wealthy, kept her under tight supervision and was her constant companion. He loaded her with gifts and treats. They spent their summers travelling together, their winters in his lavish town house. Driven by his own unconscious jealousy, he did not permit her to go out with men of her own age, and Ellen consequently developed an intense feeling of ambivalence, of sexually tinged attachment and simultaneous resentment and hate towards her overpowering father. Thus it was not surprising that she should have married a man nearly as old as he. It was easy to see that she had diverted all her suppressed resentment against her father onto her husband, who pampered and spoiled her much as had the former. From the loneliness of this pent-up aggression she had retreated into the even deeper one of psychotic withdrawal, and she did not recognize her husband because unconsciously she did not want to.

When one day I attempted very gently—on the basis of her dreams and other enlightening unconscious material —to clarify these psychic mechanisms for her, to point out the forbidden sexual overtones of her feelings and her consequent drive to escape and to punish herself, she rose from the couch abruptly.

"I understand all that," she murmured. "I'm sure you're right. Thank you. I guess I'm cured now. Thank you again."

Out she went and she did not return, although I pleaded with her and with her husband. He, however, joined with her in the belief that she did not need any further treatment and so it appeared that Ellen would be gone for good.

But six weeks later she had a new "attack" of blackout and nonrecognition. This time, after a new series of prolonged treatment with shock, she came back into analysis, bravely prepared not to leave before she stood up to her suppressed feelings and had battled down the haunting ghosts of the past.

The psychotic retreat from painful reality can proceed one step further, to a point where the break with the outside world is absolute. This emotional situation of total withdrawal is called catatonic.

One cold night in December, when the streets were thickly covered with snow, and the men and women who had returned from their jobs to their warm rooms looked pensively through the ice-covered windows at the white stillness outside, the scream of speeding fire engines momentarily troubled their snug feeling of comfort. Somewhere, something must have been going up in flames. But soon they forgot the little disturbance and returned their attention to the more significant personal events of their lives.

What had happened was, however, important. A factory had burned down, and all its thousands of costly and precious clothes—robes, dresses, jackets and costumes that had been designed, cut, stitched, sewed and manufactured there—were reduced to ashes. Since the loss was covered by insurance, the whole incident would hardly be worth mentioning, had not one of the fire fighters, protected against the flaming heat by his asbestos clothing, penetrated to a back room of the smoldering second floor, where he found, huddled in a corner, a middle-aged woman. She held a black and smoking dressmaker's dummy close to her as if it was a child, and her hand moved in a rhythmic gesture over it, back and forth, back and forth.

She was still clutching the charred dummy when the fireman, by main force, pulled her out of the flaming inferno, and later, in the hospital, she resisted with surprising strength all the attempts of the doctors and attendants to take the dummy from her. The stereotyped movement of her whole body never stopped; it was obvious that in her mind she was still sewing and dressing the dummy.

Despite the most thorough medical care, a few days later she succumbed to the extended heavy burns on her arms, her chest and her belly, and until the moment of her death she continued her symbolic movements.

When members of the hospital's social service department investigated to find out what kind of life she had previously lived, there unrolled the pathetic picture of a lonely spinster, whose life was completely wrapped up in her daily work of stitching clothes. She never missed a day; she was always at the factory the very moment its doors opened. She sat bent over her work, silent, withdrawn and uncommunicative. She was not unpleasant; she always had a friendly and empty smile for her co-workers. Everybody liked her but nobody noticed her. After her work was done she would go home to her small apartment; she would go downstairs to buy herself some food from the grocery store, then she would climb back up the stairs again. Nobody ever knew what went on behind the closed door. She never had any visitors, there was never anybody who cared. A rumor, which could not be checked, had it that once she had had a brief affair with an older man. She had enclosed her life into herself and the searing flames could not reach her—no outside pain, no outside suffering. All that linked her to the world around her was this dead dummy, which she loved and dressed and cared for, and which was a substitute for the loving and beloved child she did not have and had not been. The dummy had become the object of all the tenderness, warmth and compassion she had never found or experienced in reality.

❖

CHAPTER SIX

No Exit

THE PITIFUL LIST of mistaken and inefficient safeguards against loneliness must be augmented by one of the most puzzling and tricky devices the human mind has ever invented: the obsession, the compulsive need to think or to do something which runs counter to one's conscious desires and even to one's will. What lies behind such behavior? The simple fact that any obsessive "must," any compulsion, whether in thought or in action, any addiction, whether to drugs, to alcohol or to anything else, basically represents the attempt to build a protective rampart against anxiety and the sense of abandonment. Obsessional thoughts or actions always have a strong symbolic component and an essentially escapist character; they are the creations of a psyche fighting desperately to free itself from the commanding grip of a sense of overpowering loneliness.

The specific character of obsessional activity is clearly apparent in the lonely men and "efficient" women who always feel compelled to discuss and talk endlessly at every party, at every convention, scientific meeting or public gathering. One often gets the impression that these fidgety or pompous people are speaking exclusively to themselves, in response to an inner compulsive pressure to prove their value to the world and to out-shout the unendurable stillness inside them.

A safe and easy way of running away from loneliness is compulsive sleeping. This is a most complete measure, a regression into the prenatal state, when the foetus surrounded by the warm walls of mother's womb was protected from all threatening and painful situations. Contemporary civilization forces everyone to lead a hectic life—one which exhausts the resources of the brain cells—and the chronic look of fatigue is typical of our time. Sleep is necessary to rebuild and re-create the tired body, but when it is used as an escape it becomes a flight from life itself. For sleep is —emotionally, although not in fact—akin to death, and in this sense is symbolic of extinction and dissolution.

Still another path of escape from loneliness, more winding and less easy to recognize, is compulsive reading. It is normal to wish to incorporate within oneself the cultural achievements of others and so to enrich one's inner being and extend one's ego boundaries. The best ideas, thoughts and dreams of all the centuries, collected in the printed volumes on library shelves, open doorways to growth and to the conquest of loneliness. The newspapers and magazines, bringing the facts and figures of reality and the dramatic descriptions of a history whose current chapter we participate in writing, provide another needed bridge to the outside world. However, as soon as reading is accompanied by compulsive tension, as soon as it loses its voluntary character, so that it is no longer enjoyed, it acquires an almost nightmarish quality and becomes a heavy yoke, an iron shackle to keep man from the freedom he needs. The compulsive reader does not read for a purpose; he is driven by an inner demanding force which he cannot escape.

This process, in all its ramifications, is most vividly expressed in a letter I once received:

"I feel an immense sense of loss and depression, which is not contingent on its contents, whenever I finish reading a book. I have read a great deal from the time I was eight or nine years old, and my reading is frequently accompanied by eating—fruit, usually.

"I involve myself greatly on some level when I read—though it is probably not a factual or information-getting one. I have very little real historical knowledge although I have read a great deal of history. I am like someone who looks at a map for its color or design rather than for pertinent geographical information.

"I have a sense of security and well-being when I am in the middle of a book and dread the diminishing pages. I read *Anna Karenina* when I was eleven or twelve years old, and when I finished it I was physically ill and was taken to the doctor.

"I have a great need to have other people share the experience of a book I have read (whether they wish it or not), and on the subway I always look over peoples' shoulders to see what they are reading. I lend books with great enthusiasm and aplomb, but shortly thereafter I get frightened and suspicious that the orphan will not be returned to me. There is safety and control in books."

The writer of this letter is a middle-aged spinster, who speaks haltingly in a low, monotonous and almost inaudible voice. She is full of fear and anxiety which are in fact covers for her intense aggression. She has never permitted a man to touch her, and she uses her profession (she is a social worker) as a convenient means of ruling others. Behind all this lies a burning battle against her intense loneliness, which neither her reading nor her work has helped her escape.

The letter indicates the obsessive character of its writer;

it seems as if the force pushing her is a panicky fear lest she lose her self-control. She does not read books for their content, but rather for something which even she admits is beyond conscious and definite awareness; she compares it vaguely with the color or design of a map. She feels a sense of loss and depression after she finishes a book and suffers from an intense insecurity and lack of control. Nothing could describe more clearly the defensive character of her compulsion, and the habit of eating while she reads makes painfully evident that what has been lacking is mother's breast and mother's love which, withheld in childhood, are sought over and over again in devious ways. This is the reason she lives such a hate-ridden, self-denying, spiteful, sterile and lonely life.

The same tragic patterns can be found in those addictions which have physical as well as psychic components. Of these, two temptations and compulsive responses are of particular significance, both because they are most common and because they are most devastating in their effects. These two—alcoholism and overeating—are closely related to one another and each is equally dangerous to the well-being and healthy functioning of the total personality. Either, in its end result, spells disaster.

At first, free choice is still possible. A woman who eats out of "nervousness," because she is worried about her new dress, the new wrinkles under her eyes, or her husband's new secretary, may gain three unnoticeable pounds in one short week. A man who has engaged in business manipulations of which his moral code does not wholly approve and which might lead him into financial or ethical trouble, or one who feels overwhelmed by the daily pressures and tensions of responsibility and mounting work, may begin to drink one or two glasses of brandy every evening. But soon comes the next overindulgence in food or the next drink, and before she or he knows what is happening, the dangerous and fateful down spiral has been set into motion; the I first wants and then must; voluntary choice is gradually lost, and the struggling ego sinks deeper and deeper into a frightful dependence, which is inevitably accompanied by both moral and physical deterioration.

The end result of this process is always the same and always tragic: instead of finding an escape from the falling shadows, the addict is swallowed up by the darkness, and at the end he has accomplished exactly the opposite of his original intention: his sense of isolation is increased rather than diminished.

Alcoholism is so dramatic in its effects and, unchecked, leads to such tragic consequences, that it tends to overshadow the eating compulsion in the public mind. But even though this latter appears on the surface to be less malign, it is in fact equally destructive. It should be fairly obvious that its result—obesity—can eventually produce the same general deterioration of the total organism as does compulsive drinking. First of all, excess fat itself has an extremely harmful effect on the tissues. In addition, it puts a severe strain on the heart, by forcing the muscle to pump beyond the threshold of its efficient functioning. Indeed, new research has indicated that in the Western world more people die of overeating than of malnutrition.

In addition to the organic self-destruction of obesity is the psychological one. The compulsive eater functions on an infantile level. His behavior is a reflection of his dependence on and violent defiance of a mother who did not give him what he had, as a child, every reason to expect: her love and her attention. In his overeating, he play-acts two roles at once. Like the little girl with her doll, he is both mother and child—the good mother who gives her child what it wants and thus saves it from loneliness and the good child who is entitled to mother's love. The growing accumulation of fat under the skin seems symbolically to create a protective wall against the world, which is anticipated and experienced in adult life, just as it was in childhood, as a perilous threat. The obese person feels a compulsive need to eat—to overeat—whenever he is tense and frightened, whether his fear is based on real or imaginary dangers. And eventually he loses what he has been searching for: he has built a rampart against a mother and a world he longs desperately to be near, he has only cut himself further adrift from the love he seeks. His loneliness is raised to an intolerable pitch.

This drive to eat has nothing to do with normal hunger, which is a purely physical sensation, arising out of the body's need to maintain a metabolic balance, to replenish its used stores of energy. The automatic maintenance of an equal metabolism is regulated by the co-ordination of glandular activity, which normally keep up a definite level of what the physiologists call homeostasis—that is, physiological balance. The eating compulsion operates in complete disregard of this self-regulating mechanism. The body does not require food—additional biochemical substances to maintain the proper metabolism—the defeated psyche needs something to hold in the mouth, and that something is actually mother's breast, for which the excessive food intake is a symbolic representation. Regression to narcissism and oral sexuality is typical in all these cases, and one can almost always assume that the obese person's bridge to the other is obstructed.

All these deformed character traits were obvious in the

case of a man whose eating habits were exposed in their daily changes to an audience of millions. Walter was a television actor, a comedian. He worked on one of the best-known and most popular programs, and gained fame not only because his artistic skill merited recognition but also because the spectacular volume of his monstrously overflowing fat demanded attention. At his thinnest, he weighed considerably over two hundred pounds. He was good-natured and childish. He loved to poke around his house—to put up shelves and put in hooks and polish his car—but his interests extended no further. As was to be expected, his sex functioned but never without anxiety. He had a booming voice, and the salvos of his roars, evoked both by his own jokes and the mediocre witticisms of the others on the program, reverberated through the expanse of his body to the faintly sadistic pleasure of the millions who watched his antics.

Walter showed a certain amount of unexpected wisdom in thus subjecting himself to the laughter of the public. Not only did he amuse them, their pleasure at his expense satisfied his own masochistic drives; and daily he challenged human cruelty by making fun of his own condition.

One day he decided not to let people laugh at him any more, but rather to turn the tables and laugh at them. He went into psychoanalysis, and as he learned to understand the emotional background of his eating compulsion, he began to decrease his food intake. He lost weight rapidly, in front of millions.

"Now that you've lost all that weight, you're not funny any more," the not-too-tactful star of the show addressed him one day while the program was still on the air. "Why don't you write a book about it?" he added maliciously.

"I am writing one," Walter answered quietly.

"Do you have a title for it?"

"*My Fat and I*," he replied. The audience in the auditorium roared, and so did the invisible millions who
watched the show. They did not realize that behind this
"joke" was a profoundly serious truth: the problem of
obesity is very rarely related to a disturbed metabolism, but
almost always has to do with the psychodynamics of the
individual.

Fat presents an even more serious problem to women
than to men, because here it is complicated and dramatized
by aesthetic considerations. So many fat women almost
make a life work out of the frantic search for the "right
diet" and the "right recipes"; every morning and every
evening they check on the hated scale; they talk endlessly
about reducing methods; they take reducing pills; they try
"passive exercise" and massages. They fall for the most
ridiculous advertisements and gorge themselves on "food
without calories." Their desperation blurs their judgment,
and they accept any fraudulent claims as salvation. The
limit of their endurance is usually under a month; for
three weeks they will spend nearly every waking hour
counting calories, taking pills and tablets and getting in-
jections, more or less harmful. Then they will give up the
whole frustrating procedure and eat twice as much as ever
before.

There is something eerie as well as saddening about all
the stories of compulsive overeating. Take as an example
the experience of the pretty young housewife whose weight
went from one hundred ten to one hundred eighty pounds
in one year and who, in desperation, entered a hospital
where she could be kept on a strict diet while her physical
condition was checked and double-checked daily. When
she left the hospital she had lost forty pounds and pre-

sumably her eating habits had been so changed that now she would be able to continue her diet by herself.

But on the very night of her return home, when the house was dark and quiet, she slipped noiselessly and carefully out of bed, so as not to waken her husband, tiptoed down the stairs to the living room, removed a five-pound box of chocolates from behind the sofa where she had hidden it several months before, tiptoed back upstairs to the bathroom, locked the door, and then ravenously devoured all the sticky candy. Her movements were furtive and hurried; she kept one ear open to make sure no one had heard her, she stuffed the sweets into her mouth so quickly that she did not even have a chance to chew them.

She had refused from the very beginning to grasp the simple fact that her problem could not be solved by diet; that it had very little to do with eating, but was related to her emotional development, which was stuck in the old childhood pattern of the hungry baby who wants to take its mother's love and breast. But the bridge of adult life can function only on the basis of a two-way traffic.

I do not exactly consider myself an alcoholic, and yet I remember as one of the most entrancing experiences of my youth the time I spent on vacation near the Rhine. I had started on the hiking trip at the old German city of Coblenz, where the Mosel River mixes its moss-green waters with the sky-blue ones of the Rhine. It was late September. The round, wooded hills on both sides of the Mosel Valley gleamed in reds, golds, greens and oranges, and a light blue mist hung over the water, half-veiling it from sight. At each turn of the winding road, a different vista of this fairyland atmosphere opened up and as I walked briskly along every few minutes brought into sight another of the quaint little villages whose names were so familiar from wine bottles, and which now became narrow streets lined by steep-gabled houses and inns, every one of which I simply had to enter in order to taste a huge ten-cent glass of the golden liquid in the place of its birth. I walked and walked, and soon the glory of the day, the blue damask of the sky and the burning gold of the hills began to mix and melt in my throbbing head with the triumphant alcohol in my blood. Going on and on in the fierce rhythm of my drunken steps, the irrationality of life began gradually to blossom with hundreds of flaming petals and leaves, and the great mystery of existence suddenly became an ecstatic reality.

Does this mean that one must drink in order to be happy? That life without liquor cannot be enjoyed, that artificial stimulation is necessary because without it life has no value? I cannot accept that, and I hasten to say that the transcendent incident I just described was not the only one I have experienced; there have been many others of no less splendor, no less depth—both of joy and suffering—which did not need the gilded help of any artificial stimulus.

The fateful question here relates less to the thing in itself than to an attitude: Is drinking merely a pleasure, is it chosen voluntarily and in inner freedom, or is it used —or rather misused—as a compulsive addiction for a purpose beyond and alien to its pleasurable content?

It might be enlightening here to quote the statement of a young married couple who were addicts—not of alcohol, but of marihuana. Although each kind of addiction has, to a certain degree, its own specific psychological structure, although there are important fine differences between the

alcoholic and the drug addict, nevertheless the basic pathological trends behind addictions are always the same.

"Why shouldn't we smoke the stuff?" these people said
with a kind of accusing anger, anticipating my objections.
"Why not? We feel much better; things otherwise dreary
and boring acquire a kind of glow. It's as if they were
burning in melted copper. And our sex functions in a much
more exciting way, too, much more intense, much
more . . ."

"Unreal," I interpolated.

"That might be. But why not? What's wrong with unreality as long as it works and it's so much more thrilling?"

"The question is why you need it at all," I replied. "Why
isn't there a thrill without it?"

"That I don't know. That's your business to decide, not
mine," the woman snapped, now in open defiance, obviously as a result of her guilt. And, trying to ease it, she
added in exculpation: "And besides, we're not alone. A
whole group of us in Connecticut—seventy or eighty—we
all do it, and we all like it. *Basta cosi!*"

This tense outbreak revealed two main features which
are characteristic of every addict, irrationality as a guilt-
charged escape and the drive for company as a means of
avoiding isolation, which is experienced as a threat.

This irrationality, which might well be called neurosis,
is always present in the alcoholic, and it is this that makes
the difference between the social drinker and the addict. In
other words, it is the psychological structure of the individual rather than the organic chemical effect of the
alcohol or the drug that sets into motion the dangerous
and so often fatal chain reaction. The alcoholic is a neurotic who reacts violently to the effects of liquor, which he
experiences as gratification of old infantile drives: his oral

needs, his thirst for security and self-esteem and, at the same time, his masochistic, self-destructive character. (Notice, by the way, how closely these drives parallel those in the other compulsions.) Above all, of course, it seems to the alcoholic that liquor will help him out of his self-imposed loneliness. Thus, the question of how much alcohol any given person should drink can never be answered generally, but only in terms of his specific personality. More or less total abstention should be advised in cases in which it seems that alcohol has a specific meaning for the individual, bringing him the fulfillment of archaic, infantile wishes.

How to recognize the potential alcoholic before he is lost and caught in the vicious circle of his alcoholic compulsion? There are certain distinguishing marks. The potential alcoholic has a weak ego and cannot stand any kind of tension, frustration or waiting; he is easily overpowered by his instincts, and drifts with every wind of life. He is easily seduced and easily defeated. Psychologically, he has never progressed beyond earliest childhood and infancy, periods during which frustration is experienced as physically painful as well as emotionally distressing, and during which the inner spasticity that accompanies hunger impatiently demands relief from a mother who is hated and bitten if she does not give her breast immediately. This narcissistic lack of consideration for the needs and sufferings of others, coupled with a blurred conception of reality, this regression to an infantile state of oral sexuality and chronic tension, are characteristic of all those whose personality structures make them likely to become true alcoholics.

Never having broken away from the early stage of development in which the mother was still the sole deliverer of needed supplies, they experience the whole world as an extension of that childhood image, and see objects and people only in terms of their usefulness. This adult infant is not interested in the personality or desires of his wife or his friends or anybody else at all; he is not interested in giving pleasure or happiness to others, he is interested only in himself and his gratifications. It is not surprising, then, that loneliness is always the tragic stigma of these persons. To escape it, they scramble to bars to get drunk with others who suffer from the same loneliness. The latent homosexuality behind this desperate move is not difficult to sense. And in nearly all these cases one is confronted with the same history: of the necessity for the little boy to turn away from his forbidding mother towards a softer, more gentle father. But mother is not forgotten; the hate and fear her son feels for her remain and become his strongest bond to her and, in a later extension, to the surrounding object world. The escape into narcissistic and infantile drinking, then, symbolically represents the re-enactment of the early dawn of the victim's childhood.

After the elation of the alcoholic escape is over, the original problem of frustration appears again—this time heightened and increased—and now it takes more liquor to get the desired effect. This psychological fact is reinforced by the physiological and chemical effects of alcohol on the body. The body cells of the heavy drinker seem to require more and more of the poisonous liquid because of some chemical change in their structure, the nature of which science does not yet fully understand. The autonomic nervous system seems also to be affected by alcohol; this explains why the withdrawal process is so painful.

The alcoholic has but one interest in his world. The only thing that remains to him is a single-minded concentration and dependence—like the infant's—on the delivery of the supply. His behavior provides an indication of the degree to which this infantile regression has taken place. Does he still maintain some contact with the object world—even if this contact is an evidence of his latent homosexuality, showing itself in his noisy and play-acted conviviality with others—or has he given up such contact completely, has he disintegrated into utter narcissism, spending his lonely hours in company only with his hidden bottle? If so, he will be more difficult to influence and to cure.

The childhood blocking of normal development found in alcoholics leads to chronic pressure and tension, which may only require the reinforcement of a painful situation or some kind of seduction to come to the point of explosion.

Such was the situation of a young man who sailed one day for a trip to Europe with his attractive wife. Although he was a rather timid and withdrawn person, he was considered a successful, sober and reliable citizen, and his marriage had gone on smoothly for several years in mutual trust, fidelity and devotion. On the boat the couple made the acquaintance of a spoiled and dashing young film actor. He was broad-shouldered and handsome, an unscrupulous and habitual philanderer for whom love-making was merely a sport—with no meaning beyond this. Emotions which normally develop slowly over a relatively long period of time grow at a vastly accelerated and condensed tempo in the boredom and intimacy and unreality aboard ship. With nothing to do but eat, drink, dance or stare lazily at the empty horizon, every distraction suddenly looms out of all proportion, every stimulus is avidly received, and slumbering sensuality jumps to rapid heights, as plant growth in a hothouse. Usually, the more or less irrational involvements that are formed end when the coast comes into sight, and the bondages of true confessions, eternal friendships and flirtations dissolve under the mundane reality of the landing formalities.

When the boat docked, the actor realized with a triumphant satisfaction that he held the young woman's convulsed heart in his hand. He had given her the address of his hotel, high up in the Austrian Alps, and had suggested that she might come to visit him there—alone. The spark fell as if on a pile of dry leaves. For five days after her arrival in Europe, the wife tried to suffocate the flame that was burning away her virtue, her devotion and her responsibility to a husband who had never hurt her. For five days she could not sleep, her body tormented by an inflamed fantasy.

Finally she could not stand it any longer and she confessed. Embarrassed and guilty, she tried to minimize the depths of the passion that was shaking her. She would go away only for a few days. All this had no meaning and was only the whim of a silly woman. It would do him a lot of good to have a short vacation from her. After all, she was not the easiest person to get along with, moody and emotional. She wouldn't be able to enjoy herself for one minute if she felt that he was not happy, that he did not understand.

No, he'd be all right, he mumbled, stunned and shocked. When she left a few minutes later, the wheels of her car screeching over the hard, yellow sand of the hotel driveway, he felt a choking sensation in his throat and a picture flashed through his mind: he was lying in front of that car and she was driving straight over his body.

Numb and dazed, he went back to the hotel, asked for a bottle of whiskey and went to his room. He knelt down beside the bed. The pillow still held the imprint of her beloved head. He had only one feeling and one desire: to do something to end a pain that was beyond endurance. His head was spinning. He opened the bottle and swallowed its bitter contents in one draught. It burned his throat, but soon he began to feel better. He fell asleep and did not wake until the gray and smutty light of morning came through the drawn curtains. Squinting, he felt nothing but a piercing headache. He tried to get up. His feet were heavy and his tongue dry and white in his burned-out throat. Automatically, he stretched out his hot and trembling hand towards the bed beside him. And then abruptly memory returned. A new wave of despair and anguish threw him back onto the pillow. He rang the bell and ordered another bottle of whiskey. The day ended just as had the one before.

The following noon, his wife arrived, pale, full of embarassment and guilt. The two days had held nothing but agony, and her infatuation had died quickly under the brutal hands of a "lover" for whom this was a routine game, who was concerned only with his own lust, who had neither tenderness nor affection.

Tired and disgusted with the false pretense of a passion that had dissolved into nothing in such a short time, she took his poor gray and swollen face into her hands and kissed it. She threw her arms around him and held him to her as a mother holds her sick child. He began to cry, wordlessly, ceaselessly. After an hour he seemed quieter. He felt thirsty and rang for the waiter to bring another bottle of whiskey. She objected. He grew angry, bitter and self-pitying. She felt stunned, remorseful and guilt-ridden and the scene that followed set the pattern for many others.

When the couple went back home, everything was changed. He arrived late to work nearly every day and finally he was fired. He looked for another job; not finding one immediately, he began the long trip down that well-known road of sorrow, drinking more and more, spending hours in bars while his frightened and unhappy wife waited through the nights for his arrival. When finally he came home, he was nearly always drunk and dishevelled, often bleeding as a result of a brawl he had gotten into in one of the cheap places he frequented. Here was a sad and vengeful reversal of the roles husband and wife had played in Europe, during the two agonizing days he had waited for her in despair, when only the bottle of whiskey had helped him live through the tormenting hours. A divorce ended the first act of this tragedy.

When I finally saw him, it was evident that nothing but hospitalization would help. After that, an attempt was made to get him to understand the neurosis which had made him ripe for this tragic harvest. He made some temporary progress; his infantile behavior stopped for about two weeks, and he advanced to playing the role of the "good boy." Then he fell back into his old pattern.

I finally suggested that he join Alcoholics Anonymous, and there he found the support he could not give himself even with psychotherapeutic help. This loosely knit organization, which has no officers and is made up of ex-alcoholics from every walk of life, is very often quite helpful. A.A. members visit their recruits whenever they are needed; they can always be counted on for support when a new member feels the compulsive need to take to the bottle again. They encourage him to greater self-confidence by their own example of success in licking the evil. They try to interest him in the values of the world around him, they help him to find a job, to make contact with others—in other words, to reorganize his social life.

Why should A.A. succeed where therapy and professional assistance so often fail? In large measure because A.A., by its very nature, forces the alcoholic out of loneliness into a social world. True, A.A.'s is a symptomatic treatment, which does not pretend or hope to cure the disease of alcoholism by going to its roots. But within its limitations it has helped innumerable people to break free from their tragic loneliness and to give up a life that is useless, sterile and unbearable. The questionable enjoyment of an old infantile pattern of dependence, which to some extent is found in A.A., is still less destructive than is the thirst that can never be quenched, the thirst for something out of the past, a symbolic, unreal and hopeless yearning for a mother who was not around when she was needed.

Any improvement, any kind of cure, even in a limited form, means liberation from dependence and so at least opens the door towards growth and eventual emotional maturity. The alcoholic, like the infant, is a slave of his needs, he has no freedom of will, he cannot make decisions on his own. He knows that he is sinking ever deeper but he believes that he cannot do anything about it.

I do not know if there are any reliable statistics on the number of crimes committed under alcoholic blackout of the higher and controlling centers of the brain. Nor if there are statistics on the misfortunes that result from alcoholism: the number of accidents that occur; the seductions and unwanted pregnancies that take place; the diseases that are acquired; the friendships that are broken;

the marriages that end in divorce. But I know that the whole sensitive apparatus of society is shaken by this dreadful affliction, as by an earthquake. Nor is this the only reason that alcoholism is so dangerous. Tragic as are its effects for those who are caught in its net, even more fateful are its potentialities and repercussions for those who have to deal with alcoholics—as friends, relatives, husbands, wives, children. Time and again I have seen their suffering, in eternal worry, in sleepless nights, in victimization by daily scenes of violence and vulgarity, in obscene talk and threats of bodily harm. Those who are close to alcoholics try desperately to be helpful, yet they are soon condemned to stand by paralyzed as the tragedy becomes even darker, and the race into the abyss is accelerated. Nothing is more demoralizing than to have to witness this process of deterioration and feel utterly impotent to change its course.

Worst of all are the effects of alcoholism on children who have been compelled to watch in mute terror as the drunken father beats or rapes the mother, to listen to the insane screams of fury and petrified anguish, which break the child's life by throwing its delicate emotions into utter confusion.

Still another question must be considered. Are the genes of the alcoholic affected? Does his illness take a toll on his child's constitutional inheritance? I would not hesitate to assume that some genetic effect must exist after my experience in seeing the results of post-mortems performed on alcoholics. Practically every organ of the body is affected: the liver, the kidneys, the spleen, the brain, the stomach and the walls of the arteries—each tissue shows pathological changes, signs of degeneration and irreparable damage. Beyond the spectacular emotional regression of alcoholism are the bodily changes it produces, the bio-chemical and physio-electric effects of the drug itself, and these spell final doom and death for the organism.

We cannot leave this somber road of slow suicide and haunted error without mentioning an even more appalling picture: combined alcoholism in husband and wife. Although this kind of complicated involvement and neu-rotic teamwork is not too common, it leads to disastrous possibilities which are illuminated in the following ex-ample.

Ed was a journalist of unusual talent. His command of words was exceptional and his style often stunning and daring. Fortunately, this originality, a bit beyond the usual conservative quality of newspaper writing, had finally paid off. After years of servile compromise, he finally was given the much desired gift of his own column. Now he could at least write something of what he wanted, he could use his gift of ridicule to castigate, attack and criticize the structure of the social and political world in general and his own personal adversaries in particular. Of course, the column was not what he really wished for. Like so many other journalists and critics, Ed was a frustrated novelist and playwright, and since this dream was never realized— several manuscripts had been returned to him in polite re-fusal—he now had the ideal instrument through which to express his hate and to retaliate for the injuries done to him. Behind the façade of toughness in his writing and his behavior was the infantile structure of a much deeper frustration which he had experienced in childhood in his relationship with his mother, a domineering, masculine type whose harshness had frightened and confused him to such an extent that he was unable to establish a satisfactory emotional and sexual identification as a man.

The seductive spark which started his drinking was provided by the highly charged, tense atmosphere of the
editorial office. The deadline that has to be met, the sudden changes and cuts which must be made at the last
moment, the abruptly blocked energies, the story that refuses to be written, the often unsuccessful struggle against
the dictatorial commands of the editor-in-chief or the
owner—all these were for Ed the repetition of his childhood fight against the authority of his overpowering
mother. His earlier flight to his softer, more artistic father
and to his younger brother, with whom he had shared a
bed and enjoyed childish sex play, was reflected in his
current get-togethers with his colleagues and other writers
—critics, editors and journalists—in a well-known restaurant from which women were all but barred and in which,
in an atmosphere of purely masculine relaxation, these
men could release their tensions, loneliness and frustrations in an alcoholic conviviality that was accompanied by
another oral gratification, the endless talking and debating
that continued into the late hours of the night.

These unconscious fear reactions were the only signs of
Ed's latent homosexuality; he appeared on the surface to
be extremely masculine and, since puberty, had collected
women. He loved to seduce them and to conquer them.
Yet although he displayed the attitude of the superman, he
always felt a great strain of anxiety during intercourse. He
married several times, but all his marriages terminated in
divorce. And then one day he met a girl who, he felt, was
the answer to his dreams.

She was a young, pretty chemistry student who appeared
to be full of life and charm. But Ed's sensitive unconscious
had picked a girl of the same pattern his previous wives
showed: Carol was an anxious woman, on the border of

psychosis, who had piled up inside herself a screaming amount of hate and aggression that was the logical consequence of the vicious nagging and the unconcerned rejection she had known from both her father and her mother. The parents were sanctimonious and puritanical; they told her sex was dirty, boys were not to be trusted, her own sexual impulses were indecent and should be fought down. The child, utterly shaken in her trust, seeing herself as an unloveable and a worthless piece of dirt, fought back with fantasies of murder which in turn produced a guilt feeling which, in a vicious circle, increased her anxiety and hostility to the breaking point—the point at which only a touch was needed to push her off the brink.

The expected happened in a short time. With the oversensitivity of the neurotic, Carol soon realized that her husband was by his own personality structure unable to give her the love she had always longed for, that his behavior with her was merely a repetition of the pattern of treatment she had gotten from her parents. She began to drink, too. Unwilling to yield, sexually or otherwise, her stubborn resistance and phallic aggression re-created in him the unsuccessfully repressed image of his sadistic mother. And so the battle was on, hopeless, irrational and drowned by both in the alcoholic help-for-none.

Thus began the tragic spiral of deterioration: their gifts, their social and professional chances and their mutual dependence plummeted, and simultaneously the sadistic hate born out of disappointment and frustration mounted to an alarming height. Both of them were drunk a good deal of the time and the scenes increased in violence. Blood began to flow from the fist fights, the scratches, the brutal and beastly beatings, and the beclouded brains hurled at each within himself. He did not really see anybody. He would rush into a taxi and drive to a restaurant in the company of a few of his closest friends. Then the revival would take place, the gradual return to company and social life. He would order a huge meal and gulp down one stein of beer after another until things began to spin. There was something compulsive in all this; it was as if he had to drown the flames that would otherwise burn him to death.

When he went home, dizzy and in a mood of artificial exultation, he would sleep long and deeply, and the next morning he would again be the civilized and outgoing "good boy." During his periods of relative relaxation he was never tempted to drink to excess—until the next time and the next period of rehearsals and orgastic performances that determined the strange rhythm of this lonely yet eminently fulfilled life.

Part Three: The Conquest

✖

CHAPTER SEVEN

The Chosen Ones

AND SO IT seems that man is born alone and remains alone, and that all his spasmodic and desperate efforts to tear away the suffocating boundaries of his self only lead into deeper darkness, into error, deception, sickness, crime, guilt, and death. The goal toward which his yearnings strain is never reached, and the loneliness he seeks to escape imprints itself on him in burning letters of pain and horror. In only a few cases does the road lead up the winding staircase rather than down; up from the biological twilight of the cellar, beyond the must and misery of social entanglements, to an attic of freer breathing and royal redemption.

First among the redeemed are the artists, that very small and very important band of men and women who, in a precious and unique emotional process, are able to break the shackles. Their pangs of self-liberation give mankind its freedom; by blending the world of objects and reality with their own spiritual features they throw man's image back into the dark and unknown waters of the mystery around.

Society may scorn these chosen few, distrust and sneer at them as impractical dreamers, but this surface contempt cannot hide its envious regard. Even in our own country, with its emphasis on worldly success, on technology and "know-how," people recognize and attempt to emulate the artist's ability to liberate himself through his creative work, and in the last few years a trend has developed which aims to extend artistic self-deliverance to everyone. Men and women who are bored with the emptiness of their emotions, or are afraid of them, or who do not know what to do with the surplus of their aggressions, or who just feel lonely and shut in for any one of the many reasons described earlier in this book, have begun to borrow from the example of those chosen few, who, blessed with the gifts of talent and a special personality make-up, are the only true artists. Everyone within easy reach of a pencil and a pad of paper has become a "writer." Those few who have not sat down to bang out the great American novel on their typewriters have refrained always because they "haven't the time," never because they "haven't the talent or the need." Ballet and theatrical schools are over-crowded. Thousands happily paint away in art schools, inviting their friends and relations to visit and admire the products of their "artistic" activity at exhibits and open-ings at which the cocktail party spirit prevails, at which only a few of the guests find the time to make appropriate comments about the abstractions cluttering the walls, which might have some value as wallpaper designs, but are presented as examples of a new art.

Unquestionably, the occupational self-therapy involved in such activity has its merits, for the relatively normal as well as for the emotionally ill. Psychiatry makes use of this technique in any number of ways, and every mental hospital has its occupational therapy department. Dipping a brush into a container of paint and smearing it around in horizontal, vertical or curved lines can produce release from inner tension. The much-advertised musical self-expression, in the attack on a piano, which cannot defend itself against the hands that have decided to pound on it, is good and helpful for those who are in need of it. But the time has come to turn the stop signal on all those dilettantes who, without self-criticism, delude themselves into the belief that in their "creative activity" they have borrowed some of the glitter from the haloes that flow around the pale and suffering heads of the few truly chosen ones.

What is the psychodynamic make-up of these chosen few? How do they differ from the rest of humanity? Although these creative personalities show great variations among themselves, they do have a common denominator. Their most spectacular quality (and the plane on which all the diverse types meet) is their intense awareness of their loneliness, an awareness deeper and more poignant than that which most people experience. The artist is more shut in, more given to sensitive inner inspection, and the seismographic trembling of his emotions has a wider radius and a finer differentiation. Nor is this contradicted by the fact that he may be noisy and uncontrolled in his behavior; his surface boisterousness is merely a protective varnish designed to cover his delicate and daydreaming sensuality.

The writer, the poet, the novelist, the dancer, actor, sculptor or musician—each one is the austere and exclusively devoted servant of his loneliness. It becomes the center of his very existence. Although it cannot be artificially induced, it is often accentuated by some special suffering, like Beethoven's deafness or Chopin's tuberculosis. One can sense the pain in this letter of Chopin's: "I feel alone, alone, alone, although I am surrounded . . ." Or Beethoven's deeply moving passage in his Heiligenstadt

Will: "I was compelled early to isolate myself, to live in loneliness."

Skimming at random through the letters, autobiographies and notes great artists have left, one always finds at the bottom some such anguished outcry. Guy de Maupassant wrote: "All our strivings, our efforts, the impulses of our heart, all the cries from our lips, all our embraces are in vain, all in vain . . . we are always lonely." There is Flaubert's letter to his mother: "Contact with the world, with which I have been steadily rubbing shoulders now for fourteen months, makes me feel more and more like returning to my shell." There is Franz Kafka's more subtle letter to Milena, breathing the hopelessness of his loneliness: "Sometimes I have the feeling that we are in one room with two opposite doors and each of us holds the handle of one door, one of us flicks an eyelash and the other is already behind his door, and now the first one has but to utter a word and immediately the second has closed his door behind him and can no longer be seen. He's sure to open the door again, for it's a room which perhaps one cannot leave. If only the first one were not precisely like the second, if he were calm, if he would only pretend not to look at the other, if he would slowly set the room in order as though it were a room like any other; but instead he does exactly the same as the other at his door; sometimes even both are behind the doors and the beautiful room is empty."

There is Thomas Wolfe's mournful complaint: "The eternal paradox is that if a man is to know the triumphant labor of creation, he must for long periods resign himself to loneliness and suffer loneliness to rob him of the health and confidence, the belief and joy which are essential to creative work. . . . He knows that dark time is flowing other accusations, reproaches, recriminations and those words of naked hate calculated to hurt the most.

One night, at the height of a battle, he flung a heavy wooden chair at her. It hit her on the left temple. She grew white and without a word crumpled to the floor. Frightened and suddenly sober, he called a doctor, who, on his arrival, could only shake his head. She was dead. Ed could not believe it. He could not stand the idea of a trial, of the guilt of what he had done. He turned against himself the murderous aggression that had hit the shadow of the mother behind the wife and, after scribbling his last wish on a sheet of paper: "I want to be buried in the same grave with her," he took an overdose of sleeping pills.

Thus ended this modern alcoholic version of the Romeo and Juliet story, in which love pursued love and hate and murder became its lonely end.

One last word should be added about the use of alcohol in an attempt to quench a special form of the thirst of loneliness: the loneliness of fame. "The presidency of the United States is the loneliest job in the world," Harry Truman wrote in his memoirs. Perhaps his vigorous morning march gave him the necessary outlet; apparently he did not need to drink to excess in order to avoid his isolation.

I am not speaking of statesmen, however, but of the artistic man, the writer, singer or actor who has grown over the heads of people into a loneliness in which those who should be beside him have become an audience around him. I have known and studied many artists—men and women of great fame. I have watched their gestures and masklike faces as they gave their autographs to silly teen-agers. And I have registered their confessions of contemptuous isolation on and off the analytic couch. It seems to me that the attitude of one of these great men of the stage, who became my admired friend and whom I had the rare privilege of watching closely in all his habits and behavior, is characteristic of the whole group.

This tall, heavy-boned, handsome, middle-aged European led a very ordinary life most of the time. He ate and drank normally; he loved his wife and his children. He had friends and interests and was outgoing and earthy, full of a healthy and sensuous laughter. But one could feel the sensitivity and inner silence that hid behind the peasant façade.

At the beginning of rehearsals, only a few short weeks before his stage appearance, the preparation and transfiguration began. First came a gradual retreat into a kind of inner sanctum. He became an ascetic, abstaining almost completely from food, drink, sex, and all of the conviviality he had previously enjoyed to the brim. Something of the monk began to radiate from him then. He seemed to be in a kind of sublime loneliness; he allowed in his dressing room no one but his closest friend. And even with him the actor showed a somewhat haughty and silent tension. On opening night he would accept the applause of the intoxicated audience as a deserved tribute; although he was faintly contemptuous he himself had skillfully provoked their acclaim because he needed it. Yet when he returned to his dressing room, he felt empty and depressed, as after love-making. He would remove his wig and slowly wipe off his stage make-up. Stiffly he would walk through the stage exit to the street where hundreds of people, mostly young women, stretched out their hands for signatures or stared at him, clapping. He would go quickly through the routine of giving autographs, of nodding and smiling. But all the time he was distant and blasé, shut up by him like a river. The huge dark wall of loneliness is around him now. It encloses and presses in upon him, and he cannot escape. I know that at the end for us—the houseless, homeless, doorless, driven wanderers of life, the lonely man—there waits forever the dark visage of our comrade, loneliness."

And then there is Rainer Maria Rilke, whose *Letters to a Young Poet* are nothing but fifty pages of the most beautiful apotheosis of loneliness ever written. A few short quotations can give only a glimpse of the extraordinary delicacy with which he describes his innermost needs and the untouchable sanctuary of his loneliness: "You should not be without my greetings at Christmas," he writes to another young poet, "in the middle of the holiday, when your loneliness is even heavier than usual. But when you feel how heavily it oppresses you, be happy; ask yourself what kind of loneliness would it be had it no greatness. There is only one loneliness and it is huge and hard to carry, and to everyone comes the hour when they would like to give it up in exchange for some banal and cheap communion, for some image of a small consent with any person, even he who least deserves it. . . . But it may be that these are just the hours in which loneliness grows, for its growing is painful, like the growing of little boys and of spring. . . . Only this one thing is necessary: loneliness, great inner loneliness. Going into oneself and not meeting anyone for hours—that is what one must be able to do. Being alone as one was as a child, when the grown-ups walked about, linked with things that seemed important and big because the grown-ups looked so busy and because one did not understand what they were doing. And when the day comes that one understands how poor are their occupations, how frozen and unrelated to life their professions, why should one not see them as something alien?

For alien they are, when viewed from the depths of one's own world, from the vastness of one's loneliness, which in itself is toil and order and vocation. Why should one exchange a child's wise not-understanding for defense and contempt when not understanding means being alone while defense and contempt mean participation in a world one hopes, precisely through his loneliness, to cast off. . . ."

This scroll of the artist's loneliness could be enlarged ad infinitum. In Michelangelo and Strindberg and Dostoyevsky the cry can be heard in all the shades and nuances of the broken prism. Only one more prototype should be added, a singular artistic personality, Bertolt Brecht, who died only a short time ago and whose work is now undergoing a great rebirth, both here and in Europe. The current appreciation and revaluation of Brecht is not at all accidental. His philosophy of utter loneliness, of bitter aggression and denial, fits our time with a frightening accuracy; his pessimistic extremism opens to view the gaping abyss at the edge of which humanity stands. "The infinite isolation of man makes enmity an unattainable goal . . ." he cries out. "But communication with animals is also impossible. . . . Language is not enough for communication. . . . I have watched the animals. Love, the warmth of bodily nearness, is our only comfort in the dark. But the union of bodies does not bridge the gap in language. And yet we come together to create beings who will stand beside us in our hopeless isolation. And the generations look coldly into each other's eyes. If you stuffed a ship to bursting with human bodies there would be such loneliness in it that they would all freeze."

Another poem hardly needs comment; it is one of the most tragic and gripping love songs ever written because

there seems to be no bridge over the river of loneliness
to other human beings, not even to a beloved woman:

> . . . Und fragst Du mich, was mit der Liebe sei?
> So sag ich Dir: ich kann mich nicht erinnern.

> Doch ihr Gesicht, das weiss ich wirklich nimmer
> Ich weiss nur mehr: ich kuesste es dereinst.

> Und auch den Kuss, ich haett ihm laengst vergessen
> Wenn nicht die Wolke dagewesen waer
> Die weiss ich noch und werd' ich immer wissen
> Sie war sehr weiss und kam von ober her.[2]

From even these few quotations, it is clear that all of
Brecht's figures have a kind of shadowy, stiff, masklike
quality, and that the "infinite interchangeability of human
beings" is to him a fundamental axiom.

The attitude of this merciless poet and playwright is, in
variations, the basic approach of every artist. It is both a
philosophy and a neurosis. Babbitts are never lonely.

When the psychiatrist examines drawings done by
patients who have never painted before, he is often struck
by their artistic quality. It would seem that the neurotic
and the artist follow the same process in creation, and that
the artist is a successful neurotic, who conquers his loneliness through the creative process.

As a matter of fact, the two groups have several trends
in common. The neurotic is an adult who is stuck in his
childish attitudes; he is regressed to an earlier stage of
development. He is narcissistic and extremely self-involved.

[2] And if you ask what happened to my love/ I'll tell you: I can't re-
member/ I really know her face no more/ I only know that I kissed it
once/ And even that kiss I would have long forgotten/ Had not that cloud
been there/ The cloud I still know and will always know/ It was very
white and came down from above.

Writers, dancers, actors, musicians, sculptors, and painters show this same infantile behavior structure. They are superstitious and have all kinds of magical beliefs. They may even show some delusional trends. Most often they are exhibitionistic and regressed to an oral level, as evidenced in their characteristic love for eating, talking and kissing. Malcolm Cowley, in *The Literary Situation*, describes the writers he has known: "The writers . . . are sometimes more depressed than 'normal' persons—whoever those may be—but at other times they are more than normally elated. They laugh more than the business people I know. They like to have parties at which they eat very well, with lots of wine at dinner, talk excitedly about persons and places, flirt and flatter, play word games and late in the evening they like to dance—if they are under fifty; sometimes the older ones dance too. Often they merely talk. Young and old, they are usually good talkers, which means they are also good listeners; they get attention because they give attention."

At base, the artist is a lonely egocentric; in the creative process he utilizes the outside world to increase his own narcissistic pleasure. At the same time, through his creation, he attempts to break out of his loneliness and aloofness into what Hanns Sachs has called "the community of daydreamers."

The artist's personality structure, like the neurotic's, is so organized that the proportions of psychic energy divided among the conscious directing center (the ego) and the unconscious mass of the instinctual and emotional heritage (the id) is skewed in favor of the id. However, in contradistinction to the psychotic, who is completely dominated by his instinctual drives, the artist is not; his ego still directs and pushes the process of liberation. The

neurotic is always propelled by his unconscious into behavior which neither satisfies nor frees him. The artist,
too, is directed largely by his unconscious. But, as opposed
to the neurotic, he does achieve release through his creative work.

"Often the public forms an idea of inspiration," writes
Jean Cocteau, "that is quite false, almost a religious notion.
Alas, I do not believe that inspiration falls from heaven.
I think it rather the result of a profound indolence and of
our incapacity to put to work certain forces within ourselves. These unknown forces work deep within us, with
the aid of the elements of daily life, its scenes and passions,
and when they burden us and oblige us to conquer the
kind of somnolence in which we indulge ourselves like
invalids who try to prolong dreams and dread resuming
contact with reality, in short when the work that makes
itself in us and in spite of us demands to be born, we can
believe that this work comes to us from beyond and is
offered us by the Gods." And André Malraux follows the
same idea with the claim, that art's purpose is *"pour recreer
le monde selon les valeurs de l'homme qui le decouvre . . .
pour une negation souverain de l'ephemere . . . pour
figurer le surhumain par l'humain. . . ."*

Again here is the concept of the supernatural: that the
artist is produced by some blissful gift from heaven and
that, consequently, psychological speculation as to his
nature and the nature of his work is futile. The supposi-
tion that the artist is created by some kind of preferred
treatment encourages the neurotic belief that it is the
metaphysical father's greater power that speaks through
the helpless son. The artist, as acting representative of God,
is no longer responsible for what he creates. The impulses,

wishes and fantasies of his unconscious, which he exter-
nalizes in the work of art, are attributed to a supernatural
being, and the creative process by which they become
conscious is described as an action of this transcendent
entity. And so activity is transformed into passivity, and
again one is back in neurosis; the fantasies are centered
around the parent and around the conflict between active
and passive sexual tendencies in the individual and their
sublimation. One is reminded of Michelangelo's poem:
"Hammer me down, God! Hammer me down, Hammer-
God!"

What, then, motivates the artist? Like everybody else
he is driven by the need to get out of his loneliness, to
relieve the tension that inevitably accompanies his feeling
of anxious isolation.

This anxiety of loneliness oppresses man's life from the
beginning. The newborn baby, with his undeveloped and
untrained senses is threatened by the unknown world outside and terrified by the impulses of his body within. The
tensions he suffers demand an outlet. He cries. And these
tears are in themselves his relief reactions. Holding them
back and finally letting them go brings him narcissistic
pleasure. The similarity to the artistic process is quite
striking: paintings and poetry are the tears of the artist.
A. E. Housman said: "If I were obliged, not to define
poetry, but to name the class of things to which it belongs,
I should call it a secretion; whether a natural secretion,
like turpentine in the fir, or a morbid secretion, like the
pearl in the oyster. . . . I think that my own case, though
I may not deal with the material so cleverly as the oyster
does, is the latter; because I have seldom written poetry
unless I was rather out of health, and the experience,

though pleasurable, was generally agitating and exhausting."

This craving for release of tension is one of the fundamental laws of life. It determines its measure and rhythm. It begins in the biological basement, and reaches its peak, high up in the attic, with art and science, which follow the same rule of piling up and dissolution. This is experienced in its purest form in music. Point counterpoint, discord dissolved into accord.

"An artist works because he must," says Picasso. And Rilke wrote: "Investigate the reasons that command you to write. Do their roots stretch into the deepest center of your heart? Confess whether you would have to die if writing was forbidden you. A work of art is good when it grows out of necessity." And Flaubert: "The writer does not choose the story, the story chooses him."

Expressed in more scientific terms, one notices that the artist feels a compulsive need to relieve his inner tensions: loneliness and guilt. This sense of inner pressure is characteristic of his personality. His aggressive eruptions—his work of art—are painfully held back until the condensation of the emotional process has found the specific form through which they can be expressed. And again it is Rilke who writes: "Actually, the artistic experience is so unbelievably close to the sexual, to its suffering and its lust, that the two are, basically, only different forms of the very same longing and bliss."

This link between art and sex—and especially homosexuality—is most vividly illustrated in the story of an attractive girl of twenty, who was for several years a gifted art student but who abruptly stopped painting after a love affair with her professor, the first man with whom she had ever experienced sexual release.

To understand this reaction and its significance it must first be noted that the young woman's personality pattern was typical of the latent homosexual. Here, as in every patient of a similar psychic structure, it developed that the child's sexual growth had been confused by the familiar situation in which the mother was masculine and domineering while the father was soft, introverted and aloof.

As in the case of the mute child described earlier in this book, I had suggested to this patient that, as an accompaniment to her analytic treatment, she make some pictures to which she would give her free associations. She started out with two revealing finger paintings. The first, she said, represented "father and mother." It showed a fat, powerful mother and a kind of skeleton father. Her associations to this picture were: "The eternal woman and the loving man." The other drawing consisted of a series of vertical lines painted in bold, blue strokes. "I pressed my finger as hard as I could. These are supposed to be trees." As she painted, I noticed that these energetic dashes were done with an aggressive violence, the arm and hand moving in the direction away from her body. Such phallic aggression showed both her identification with and her violent fight against her suppressing mother, and made clear her basic problem.

The girl had never been able to accept the fact that she was a female: to her a woman was only a castrated man, castrated by the threatening mother. To be a man, to have a phallus, thus became a necessary defense against her fear and her deeply masochistic enjoyment of it. The successful affair with her professor, who was obviously a father figure, made it necessary for her to give up this illusionary phallus in favor of feminine fulfillment, and thus forced her to turn against herself the aggression which had heretofore found its expression in painting. The abrupt termination of her artistic activities, then, had only one meaning: "I can create only as long as I am a man." Clinical experience seems to indicate that this young woman's latent homosexuality is characteristic for the artist; the precarious balance between sadistic-aggressive (masculine) trends on the one hand and masochistic grati- fication (feminine) on the other, is the psychodynamic basis of every creative personality.

So far, this discussion has centered on the works of the "creative" artist, the painters, sculptors, composers, and writers. But there are others in addition, the interpreters. The actor, the singer and the musician are, in a literary sense, not productive but reproductive: they do not expose their vulnerable selves to the pregnant silence of their studios and the incalculable adventures of unforeseen hours. But, with the same sensitive recklessness as the others, they serve at once humbly yet in exaltation the contriving spirit of the author or composer. They have their fixed hours of rehearsal and performance; on demand they enkindle their emotions with the help of a technique painfully and carefully studied through the years and now put to a calculated use. But this does not lower either their value or their accomplishment. The great actor and the great actress are lit by the same halo which illuminates the head of the creative artist, and the act of reproduction is hardly less consuming and agonizing than the act of production.

Yet there are differences, which must be understood. Orality and narcissistic self-enjoyment are even more im- portant to the interpretive artist than to his creative brother, and present in this regard a greater danger to him. The actor must walk the tightrope between enough narcissism and orality to make possible the necessary exhibitionism. Too self-involved, he cannot project himself into a role, cannot sympathize or empathize with any other person but himself, cannot give life to the author's character. The difference between the artist and the performer, then, is the difference between the "right" excess of narcissism and a superfluity.

The creative artist hides his actual self from view and presents his inner nakedness to the public in the sublimated medium of his creation. The actor, singer and dancer, on the other hand, look directly into the public's eye. Standing in the light of the offensive footlights, they perform their act of spiritual striptease in front of an audience whose applause gives them the atonement they need for the robbery they have committed: using the playwright's or the composer's words or music as a stagecoach for the conquest of their own loneliness. Yet, although the playwright is covered by the screen of his work, the actor can hide behind the shadow of the creative artist whose work he brings to life. Thus, he enjoys a similar protection.

"Art," wrote D. H. Lawrence, "is a form of supremely delicate awareness and atonement—meaning at-oneness, the state of being at one with the object." It is not only the artist who conquers his loneliness by his identification with his work; the audience transcends itself in a similar way. Art can be a road to the conquest of loneliness for every man.

If books, paintings, music, drama and the dance did not answer a need in everyone, they would never find a public. For the artist is only one half of the creative process; his audience is the other. To its audience, a work of art is a communication, a cry from one lonely individual that finds a liberating response in its hearer. The man who stands before the paintings of El Greco, who reads the works of Dostoyevsky, who listens to the music of Bach or Beethoven, is not merely a passive receiver of "information" or "sensations." As he actively projects himself into the work of art, as he attunes himself to its message, he engages in a kind of communication with the work itself, with its creator and with himself. Thus he conquers his loneliness by so expanding his ego boundaries that he becomes more than this isolated self; he becomes the growing repository of the total world around him, filtered through the eyes of the creative master.

The degree to which art serves its audience as a liberation from loneliness is even more striking when one considers the performing arts. The emotional effects of drama, music and the dance are often greater than those of literature and painting and even these effects are heightened when the audience is not simply a scattered collection of single individuals, but a large group. Sir Laurence Olivier's performance of Shakespeare's *Richard III* on television was impressive indeed, and yet it could not and did not have the impact on its viewers of the screen performance. For each television audience is made up of single individuals, sitting in their homes. There may be as many as ten gathered together, yet, lounging in comfortable chairs, they do not achieve the cohesiveness and unity of the larger group in the theater. Here, in the darkness, the individual is liberated from his loneliness most dramatically because he is linked with others, sharing a common experience and reaction to the world presented on the stage. Aristotle defined catharsis—the desired effect of every play—as a kind of purification, a guilt release, a liberation from loneliness that spreads down from the stage to the audience.

And so it can be seen that the performing artists serve best their function of transcendant communion, when their audience is gathered together, in the dark warmth of the theater, so that each individual can tune his receiving antennas not only to what is happening on the stage, but to what is happening in the very next seat.

Today there is a growing interest in high fidelity recordings, which bring the greatest works and the greatest performances of master musicians into everyone's home. These records are technically so perfect that they sound almost exactly like the actual live performance. Still, concert going has hardly decreased, but rather increased. Something still drives men and women from the warmth and comfort of their own living rooms to the stiff discomfort of the concert halls, where they sit—often with their eyes closed, so that they do not even see what is happening on stage—through hours of music they could as easily hear alone, in their homes. The explanation for this apparent paradox lies in the fact that man's liberation from loneliness is most complete when it is shared with the faceless, anonymous, lonely beings who surround him.

An understanding of this fact reveals both the strengths and the weaknesses, the range and the limitations, of television. As long as this technical marvel brings the individual face to face with other individuals who act on the moderate emotional key of everyday life, it establishes a valuable communication between the actor and the audience. Television is essentially an eavesdropping medium, not a participating one, and consequently it cannot help the individual to break dramatically free of the walls that encircle his frightened self. It is only partially satisfactory because it demands passivity of its audience. Since, however, this passivity is the appropriate response to quiet communication, television performs a real service when it limits itself to this soft-spoken approach.

But the stage, the theater, must be larger than life. If its events are merely a photographic repetition of reality, the effect will fail and spell disastrous boredom. The aura has to be present, the atmosphere of something that could be real but is not. If this effect is missing, there is an inevitable disappointment, which I once encountered as a result of my own misconceptions and blundering.

It happened in a small Austrian village where I was invited to watch a performance of the Christmas play. These presentations usually depict the appearance of the star to the shepherds, the story of Herod, Christ's birth, the adoration of the magi, and all the rest of the nativity legend. Here the scenes were performed in a stable and the actors were children, who ranged in age from twelve to fifteen years. Through the thin walls one could hear from time to time the melodious ringing of the bells which, of different sizes and sounds, hung around the cows' necks; one could distinguish the clanging of the chains and the rubbing of the heavy, invisible bodies against the primitive wooden planks. The dimly lit auditorium was redolent of hay and honeysuckle, whose faint odor was breathed in by a mild draft through the open door. The Holy Babe lay in an unadorned crib that a few hours before must have been used by some of the cattle on the other side of the wall.

The children had made their simple costumes with the help of their families. The twelve-year-old Herod wore a heavy blood-red cloak theatrically wound around his shoulders; the day before it had probably covered his father as he took his afternoon nap on the couch. And the thirteen-year-old Mary was dressed in an old-fashioned light blue peasant dress; the transparent veil around her fine blond hair reached down to the dusty floor. Her costume might have been the one her mother wore as a girl, when, on Sundays, she danced with the boys in the neighboring villages. The play was performed in the pale beam of the candle-footlights before dark, straight-hanging curtains. There was a naïve dignity in the restrained gestures and the moving seriousness of the children. This thirteen-year-old Mary, with her long blond hair that looked like a faint breath of floating cobwebs, did not play-act; she could actually have been the Holy Virgin in all of her innocent, prim and demure loveliness.

When, after the final curtain, I went out into the starry night, the moon was out: cold, hard and virginal. I groped my way through dark and rugged roads, lined by old, half-crippled oak trees, to the sleepy station. And I made up my mind to arrange for these children to be invited to repeat their stirring performance on the stage of the great city theater.

The arrangements were made. The performance took place. It was a complete flop. And it took me several days to realize what had happened. A play which had been a precious work of art in one frame was simply a clumsy and too realistic projection in another. The atmosphere and the audience simply could not be transplanted from a small Austrian village to the sophisticated city.

This point may become even clearer in the story of another experience with another theatrical audience. The famous Leningrad Children's Theater is unique. Everything is operated by children: the manuscript of the play and its direction, the sets and costumes and the whole technical apparatus, and, of course, the acting. The audience consists exclusively of children, except that in each wedge-shaped section of the huge amphitheater a teacher is posted whose task it is to watch the reaction of each child in his section. How many children yawn, when and how many laugh, at what point do they cry, what is their mood-swing, their degree of tension, of excitement, etc. After the first performance, the teachers get together and their detailed experience is pooled and reduced to a mathematical curve that shows the children's emotional reaction to each phase of the total play. Changes are then made in the manuscript in accordance with these results. The same process is repeated at the second performance and the manuscript is revised again until a kind of ideal reaction pattern is produced. Since I came from a different cultural atmosphere, my own reaction to these purely propagandistic and politically flavored performances was quite different from the children's. I did not feel that the plays had any more artistic value than, let's say, a cowboy film. There was a lot of shouting, big and bragging, there were criminal traitors to the communist cause, and a moony love story as a side issue. The setting, however, was expressionistic, rather tasteful and interesting. There was some attempt at a condensed style, but hardly anything else that could have aroused any enthusiasm in me, and if the teacher in my section had recorded my reaction, he probably would have marked down mostly plain boredom.

The children, however, could make an ideal identification; they were melted and forged together into one group by a performance which got the appropriate and, according to the psychological test system, best results for all. All this, to be sure, is far removed from art; it might be called a rather drab method of getting out of loneliness. But collectivism, which is believed in the communist countries to be the key for the solution of political, economic and personal problems, tries to find the answer for human misery on a mechanical level, leaving out completely the emotional needs of the still lonely and suffering individual.

This is not a conquest, but another escape. The light will not come from Lenin, but from Beethoven.

CHAPTER EIGHT

The Periphery and the Center

NOW THAT WE have left the treacherous trenches of defense, the signpost of deceit, the detours and the dead-end
streets, now that we are out of this wasteland, in the open,
we can have a clear view of the ways in which the conquest
of loneliness can finally be achieved. This conquest can
be accomplished not only by the chosen few but by all
who are willing to find and destroy two main foes and
obstacles: narcissism on the one hand and hostility on the
other. Both make it almost impossible for the individual
to communicate with the world; both keep him locked in
a death struggle with himself, unable to see or feel his
relationship with others.

The very possession of this sense of relationship, of
belonging, is one of the hallmarks of maturity. The men
and women whose emotional problems are so severe that
they require professional help have never been able—no
matter what form their specific and individual difficulties
take—to achieve strong positive ties to the world; it is
for this reason that they feel lonely, anxious, tense and
unhappy. Freud called this attachment outside oneself
"object cathexis"; by this he meant libidinal interest and
anchorage in the other—in an activity, an object, another
human being—something that leads the individual away
from narcissism and becomes so important that it is neces-

sary for his very survival. This attachment is related not only to man's biological dependence on others; it is a deeply rooted psychological need as well. It is a part of man's humanity.

The infant recognizes its meaning to him within a year of his birth. As his ego, his sense of self, develops, and as his first diffuse awareness is sharpened into a more vivid and pinpointed perception of himself and others, he begins to appreciate his emotional relationship to his small world. Here again the role of the mother is of prime importance. She is the first one with whom the child establishes a relationship, it is to her that he directs his first attachment outside himself. The pattern by which he responds to her and she to him thus becomes the model for all his future object relationships, and determines to a large extent his ability to establish meaningful communication with his world.

If the baby's bond with his mother is not strong and healthy, he is likely to retain the narcissism and self-interest of early infancy throughout his adult life; he may never succeed in breaking away from the circular, centripetal movement of early childhood. Eventually, he will be imprisoned in loneliness. His emotional status will remain on the level of infantile masturbation, without object relationship. If, on the other hand, the mother is linked to her baby by antagonism, rather than love, the infant's emotional development is similarly thwarted. Hate and aggression may become his only means of communicating with the world; the lesson he has learned at his mother's breast becomes the model for all his later relationships. Or, out of fear of this early hate, the child may withdraw into himself, into lonely narcissism. Essentially, one of these things has happened in every case of severe emotional difficulty; the adult finds communication impossible because he has never really learned it.

If, instead, the infant discovers, from a warm and gratifying relationship with his mother, the emotional satisfactions of belonging, of interests outside himself, he will be able, despite the many setbacks with which life is bound to confront him, to form rewarding attachments on many levels and so to conquer his loneliness each time it assails him.

Still, even those whose early life has prepared them for the trials of maturity can find no guaranteed formula. There is no panacea for loneliness. Man's self-awareness, his libidinal drives, his fear of death, the characteristics of contemporary society—all of these present him with problems which must be met and fought every day. It is man's destiny to battle constantly against his loneliness. This battle must be fought on many fronts. It is won only by those who can face these facts and who are willing to make a strategic retreat, at least once in a while, and to surrender themselves to this bewildering emotion on some occasions.

For as has been pointed out before, the problem of loneliness cannot be solved or conquered by running away from it. As a matter of fact—and this is spectacularly clear in the case of the creative artist—the feeling in itself must be respected and cultivated as a precious and necessary positive nucleus around which man's oscillating life is organized. The noisy clamor of civilization deceives the very sense of existence; too often man forgets that his hours of contemplation and silence, not to be confused with narcissism, present possibly the most treasured values and essentials of his life.

In some parts of India men and women of a certain age call all their relatives, friends and servants together, bid them unsentimental good-byes and then withdraw into the woods to live out the rest of their days in self-imposed meditation. This is, indeed, a great concept for a meaningful and intelligible design for living. On the other hand, I do not see any special reason why man should wait until old age for such a period of inner silence. Why should he not allow himself, nay train himself, to experience throughout all his days, a continuous undercurrent of this feeling so that it is no longer something to fear, but becomes rather the well from whose clear waters he may fertilize the aridity of his social and professional routine. And so he can link himself from the first to the last spark of the incomprehensible goings-on around him. In such a way he will get a true perspective; those small things and incidents that often bother and irritate him to the brink of destructive paralysis will finally be experienced in their relative insignificance and unimportance. He will gain an imperturbable feeling of safety, an inner knowledge that he has a kind of joyous armor around him.

A young medical student, the son of wealthy parents, spoiled and surrounded by all the luxuries civilization could provide, who was assured of a brilliant social and professional future, decided one day on a complete change for at least half a year. I could not detect any neurotic trend in him or in his desire to throw over his old life for this short period. He was just "fed up." He had been successful in school, he was popular with his pals, he had an understanding and affectionate girl friend, who loved him dearly and whom he loved with great tenderness. But he felt that the clamor and routine of his daily life were gradually drowning out the still voices within him; that his sense of himself was being lost in the buzz of professional and academic competition, the whirring noises of technology and the hectic emptiness and boredom of the parties and other social engagements he was compelled to make part of his life. He was not trying to escape any hidden ghosts in his own unconscious. He was not trying to avoid himself and his responsibilities; rather he was trying to find them and appreciate them in their true reality.

He took a pile of good books, some records and his typewriter. He left town and moved to a simple furnished room in a small fishing village. He had no telephone, no television—not even a radio. The nearest post office was two miles away. Once a week he wrote to his girl friend and once a week he received a letter from her in return. He read and wrote and walked; he listened to the cries of the seagulls and watched the ever changing tides and breathed the clear salt air with a deep joy. In the evenings he played his records or went down to the simple little inn and chatted, when he felt like it, over a glass of wine with the townspeople.

Layer after layer of something that had been weighing him down seemed to be melting away, and gradually a feeling of unstained happiness began to percolate through his entire being. When, some months later, he returned to the city, his life there no longer seemed to him oppressive. A timeless treasure and foundation had resulted from his appointment with eternity at the edge of the sea, and no convention, no small pedestrian routine of daily observances, could ever destroy this.

This story reminds one of the tragic fate of Friedrich Nietzsche, who wrote his famous *Thus Spake Zarathustra* in Sils Maria, in the sizzling blue air of the high valleys of the Swiss Engadin. Here in his sublime solitude, devoting his life exclusively to his thinking and philosophical writing, his past suddenly caught up with him. At the time when he had still lived down in the shadowy cities, he had once slept with a prostitute, who had infected him with syphilis. At the time there had not yet been discovered any drugs with which successfully to fight this pernicious disease. To the suffering Nietzsche, it seemed that the city's dirty wave of human debasement had followed him all the way to the noble and pure loneliness of his mountain retreat. His last work, *Ecce Homo,* combines the highest mental lucidity with the faltering delirium and the mad rhythms of his infected and inflamed brain, and bespeaks the tragedy of a genius who had consciously and intentionally sacrified his life to his highest loneliness.

This kind of life seems to be completely opposite to the behavior of those who try to run away from their stillness rather than to cultivate it; who need the screaming noise of their surroundings as much as they need oxygen, because they are afraid to face their own emptiness. Those who cannot retire into the teeming abyss of their selves to find the substance and the riches that hide, paradoxically, in the void, can never conquer their loneliness. They have always been too frightened to meet it face to face; never willing to expose themselves to the "disease"; they never build up an immunity to it. They run away from their own thoughts, from the delicate voices that bespeak their real selves. It seems that the characteristic gesture of our time could be represented by a man lying naked on the beach in the hot sand, the eternal waves of the sea in front of him, the wind, the clouds and the silence above him, a portable radio at his side. Squinting his eyes away from the blinding light and the vastness that surrounds him, he listens sleepily and with dissatisfied bore-

dom to a commercial jingle making its way through the
air from some studio in the dusty city to the burning bliss
of the blue high noon. He sees the sun as beauty-parlor
equipment with which to improve his health and tan his
skin and a swim in the thundering ocean as hygienic
exercise for which he does not have to pay.

Only those who can accept their loneliness as a re-
current theme and rhythm of their lives, as a positive
reality of their beings, as an essential part of their humanity, can enjoy and acknowledge, with grace, with gladness,
and without anxiety, their relations and bondages to the
other world particles around and beside them.

Still, man cannot live entirely in and of himself.
*"Menschen sind schwimmende Toepfe, die aneinander
stossen,"* Goethe remarked to his friend and biographer
Eckermann. And John Donne wrote, "No man is an island,
entire of itself. . . ." Even Nietzsche in his mountain retreat
threw a life line out from himself to the world through
the books and thoughts with which he enriched it. For
those whose genius does not lie in the solitary life, who
communicate with the world through people and objects
rather than ideas, society must offer channels through
which they can express their sense of relatedness.

Among these channels is that broad area which can be
subsumed under the general heading of religion. In this
book religion is to be discussed in psychological rather
than philosophical terms. It is not my purpose, to argue
the delicate and debatable values of one religious belief
against another. Someone once said that religion is a private
affair. It should not be commanded or suppressed. Each
man, each woman, modifies the shape and form of his or

her approach to the enigma of life in accordance with his own specific personality, his experiences, his personal and social inheritance, the culture into which he is born—the totality of his being. Indeed, the ways in which man interprets this miracle seems of less relevance than the fact that he is aware of it, and feels the need to explain it in some way. It makes very little difference, then, whether one talks in terms of the community of God's children or of a common substance that has, through millions of aeons of evolution, developed into the differing aspects of stars, animals and men. Nor do I think the name it is given is of decided importance; any one is simply a confession of ignorance.

Indeed, it is more important that one asks the question than that one finds the answer. For the simple fact that this issue is raised is the broadest, most basic and most irrefutable proof that man, unlike any other form of creation, feels the need to relate himself to the vast universe in which he has his being. No matter what specific forms his answers take, religion, the question itself is in this sense a bridge away from loneliness, a connecting link between man and his world.

"Religion is the opium of the people," Marx wrote. One reads this slogan on a wall near the entrance to Red Square, Moscow's most beautiful thoroughfare. The complex buildings of the Kremlin, which outline the square on one side, are eclipsed by a huge red flag, symbol of communist power. Lighted from beneath, it flutters in the wind like flowing blood. Only a few steps away, on the short side of the square, stands one of the city's most famous churches, a jewel of Muscovite architecture with its many colorful towers, the tops of which are adorned with onion-like caps. At the time I saw it, it was unlighted, unheated and empty; the victim of the Soviet's antireligious drive. Church services were forbidden, and inside the place looked like a dead rock canyon. It was freezing cold. A bit frightened, I groped through the misty dimness. Suddenly I almost stumbled over something shadowy and soft on the dark floor. It was an old woman, her head bent deep, touching the hard and dirty stone floor in a motionless silent prayer.

Religion, then, serves to channel that common human feeling of awe into the labyrinthine intricacies of life. It is, of course, not the only channel. The scientist, who seeks in patient and laborious experimentation to answer the basic questions of the nature of matter makes the methods of empirical proof the core of his beliefs. The law of probability is his god. What is important, however, is that the very existence of science and religion indicate man's need not merely to understand, in a dry, intellectual way, but to feel connected with his world.

Religion has important social values as well. That this is true can be seen from even the most cursory examination of the basic tenets of all modern creeds. The psychiatrist, seeking to explain the meaning of religion to man, must look beneath the forms and symbols, beneath the rituals and services which distinguish one denomination from another, to the core, the central idea around which these forms are built. There is one common denominator among the great contemporary religions of the world, one point at which all of them, no matter how great their individual differences, converge. Christianity and Judaism, Mohammedanism and Buddhism all demand the same thing of man—universal love. As a moral principle and a rule of conduct this concept has basic meaning and value, and is completely endorsed by psychiatry.

Of course, in an historical and evolutionary sense, one must assume that this ethic was originally merely a necessity, without which society could not have survived. As soon as man moved out of isolation into social groups, his instinctual drives had to be regulated; if they were not, everybody would have murdered everybody else and every woman would have been subjugated to every man's desire. The development of an ethic must, then, be looked upon as the product of a socially inevitable logic. However, notwithstanding its origin, if it is correctly understood and applied, it will finally curb the intensity of hate and aggression, which are the central black spots and curse on the road to deliverance through communication with the world.

It finds its expression not only in devotion to a god—by whatever name he is called—but in devotion to man, and in the social aspects of its practice. The church as a center for community activity provides a real bridge away from the lonely self. Increasingly, the temples and churches are beginning to recognize their social responsibilities. Increasingly, they are beginning to assume a vital role in community life and to act as centers for all kinds of social activity; to teach the values not only of their specific creeds, but the values of others as well; to help man learn more about the diversity of form and expression in which common human aspirations can be clothed. In this sense, the church or the synagogue stand midway between the individual and the community, providing a center to which each man can bring his problems, and in which each can look for solutions. The religious feeling is an indication of man's need and his ability to break away from loneliness; religious institutions are among the tools he has devised for this purpose.

However, some dangers present themselves, which must be faced. For religion can be misused; the form of religion can be substituted for its content, and religion's basic purpose—to give man a sense of relatedness to his world—can be forgotten in the struggle over details. By such confusion man has, through the centuries, set belief against belief, dogma against dogma, and our planet has been shaken and drowned in blood. The Christian knights fought the Holy Wars with the same bloody passion as did their enemies in the Arab and Islamic states. Luther's struggle against Rome is in psychological terms only a replica and repetition of the same pattern, and the Holy Cross and the Holy Crescent are only the symbols of nuances of the same human need.

This aggression and hate have been transferred from the heavenly to the earthly plane; no longer are wars waged in the name of God, but in the name of a country, of a politico-economic entity. As man has moved to a greater understanding of religion's symbolic role in life, he is no longer able to use it as a scapegoat for his hostility, and so he fights in the name of his "soil" or a certain color combination—a flag—or an arrangement of musical sounds—a national anthem, and his national "principles." For the symbols of religion he has substituted the symbols of artificial frontiers.

Religion can be used not only to cover up man's hostility and aggression; every so often it veils a special brand of narcissism and becomes an escape from loneliness rather than a tool with which to conquer it; a cozy nest into which the sufferer retreats when the problems of life become too overwhelming. All the lonesome and frightened men and women who use religion in such a distorted way simply repeat and transpose the very human situation of the neurotic from the earthly plane onto a transcendental level. They regress into childhood, into a period in which the lap of the family is needed as an island of refuge and as a weapon against dreaded isolation.

For the psychoanalyst, there is a sad fascination in recognizing the degree to which this neurotic defense can be repeated on a metaphysical level, in seeing how the same unconscious forces that motivate the neurotic can be operative in the case of the apparently "devout." For each lives in the fantasy that he is still a child, helplessly exposed to the overwhelming powers around him, and therefore in need of someone stronger: his parents.

To the neurotic believer, God has all the qualities every child attributes to his father: he is omnipotent, he is infallible, he is omniscient. Actually, every father is a god to his child and every mother a beautiful goddess, allpowerful and magically endowed. Belief in magic is characteristic of childhood, as was pointed out earlier; it remains among those who refuse to give up their childhood and who live in the present as if it were the past.

This is how the world seems to the child: the father-god has unlimited power. He can fulfill the child's every wish. He can change evil into good. He can keep all dangers away from the frightened child. He is the strongest of all and the most handsome. Never for a moment does the child doubt him. Father is concerned only with the child's happiness; the child has only to believe and not to question, and everything will turn out for the best.

And father knows everything. He has all the answers to all the confusing questions. He understands all the incomprehensible events in the child's world. He knows all the secret connections and causes and reasons. But he also knows everything about the child. Father can see behind the child's forehead and knows what he thinks and what evil and forbidden things he has done. Father is just and will punish the child, but he is also kind and forgiving and will love the child whatever sin he may have committed.

And father is all-present. He is constantly around, protecting and watching over the child, even when he is far away.

Here is the philosophy of utter dependence, the philosophy of failure, which every neurotic brings to his relationships with the world. He does not act, but is acted upon. He has no strengths, only weaknesses. He is small and frightened. He abdicates to father—or by extension to his government or his God—all the problems that he should at least be able to try to solve by himself. He does not see the symbolic meanings in many religious rituals: Holy Communion as an effort to break down the walls that separate man from man, to incorporate the life force into oneself; the Passover Seder as a symbol of the continuity of life, of the conquest of loneliness through identification with the past and with the future, so that terrorizing death becomes less of a threat. To him, these rituals have only a mechanical meaning; they are a child's magical devices to get the help he needs and wants.

Some years ago a movement was started which aimed to blend psychiatry with religion; to pool the therapeutic goals and means of both in order to ease the suffering of mankind. Many factors make such a proposal understandable. Psychoanalysts and psychiatrists are forced to charge comparatively high fees for their services, which only the privileged few can afford. Thus economics alone offers a realistic temptation to favor the blend of religion and psychiatry. In addition, the tragic fact is that there are simply not enough qualified psychiatrists to meet the needs of the thousands of more or less confused or neurotic men, women and children. Since the psychiatrist can see no more than ten or eleven patients daily, thousands are stranded and forced to carry on the unceasing and hopeless struggle to overcome and kill their ghosts and shadows by themselves. There are simply not enough trained physicians or mental hygiene clinics to give the much needed professional help. It is an attractive idea, therefore, to consider increasing the number of the healers by adding the men of the cloth to their group.

Unfortunately, I am afraid that the benefits might be smaller than the drawbacks. For one thing, the door for the many untrained and insufficiently prepared lay therapists, so far only ajar, would be pushed wide open for any kind of dilettante approach to diseases that are much more difficult to diagnose in their dangerous potentialities than are organic ones. Emotional illnesses follow definite laws. Some of them are organically conditioned. Only the psychiatrist with medical training should diagnose and treat such diseases. One wrong word might spark a fateful explosion.

Of course loneliness, which lingers in the background of most emotional disturbances, might in any case be at least partially helped by the mere fact that now an interested father figure cares, and is really interested and full of the affection and love which the childhood parents never gave. The minister and the psychoanalyst are experienced in precisely this fashion. But this transference by itself is not enough to effect real cures. A patient in analysis is not discharged until he has learned to see his doctor as a human being, not as a father figure. The psychiatrist is called upon to deal with people who are really ill, in whom loneliness is an oppressive chronic condition. His patients do not have minor complaints. They have serious diseases which require the kind of scientific treatment that can be given only by those who are thoroughly trained to cope with them. Otherwise we are inviting potential catastrophes.

Psychiatry is the most difficult branch of medicine, and it is not accidental that its training takes more time than does any other specialty.

Still, psychiatry and religion have one thing in common; the unceasing fight against hate, that scourge of humanity; the eternal, never-to-be-discouraged battle for love among mankind. Whether this suffices, whether it is enough of a common ground to keep the alliance between psychotherapy and religious therapy together, seems to be at least doubtful. For as the psychiatrist would not recommend the long, painful and costly method of psychoanalysis for someone whose problems were not severe and deep-seated, so it would be wrong for any untrained person to attempt to treat with a few well-meant words the diseases that call for deep therapy.

When I spoke of the wise old Biblical legend of the expulsion from paradise, I left out one decisive factor: God ordered Adam to work from then on. "In the sweat of thy face shalt thou eat bread." And so there was imposed on man a life in startling contrast to his previous blissful, naïve, childhood enjoyment of instinctual animalism. Mature, adult life had to begin: a life of work. It was thought of as a punishment—but perhaps it was a blessing.

"I'd like to have a money tree in my back yard," a young

man day-dreamed. "Every one of the leaves is a hundred dollar bill. I sit, leisurely dozing in the warm sun, doing nothing, and from time to time a gentle breeze sweeps the leaves right into my lap."

He did not know that his depression and his loneliness were related to this dream; he still wanted to be taken care of by his parents, instead of breaking this childhood pattern, becoming an independent adult, and getting a job.

Work, labor, activity, seem to be the natural attributes of a healthy, normal adult life. Idleness leaves man open and vulnerable to brooding and self-pity, exposed to his loneliness. Activity is both a pleasure and a responsibility; it means effort and it means movement—movement of the muscles, movement of the mind in spiritual accomplishment, movement directed away from the self.

To watch animals and children is to notice that they constantly move about, playing and running around much more than necessary. It is obvious that this movement in itself brings them pleasure, a pleasure that can grow in intensity to often absurd extremes.

When I was a young man, living alone, I had a cat as my pet. She was young, soft, playful and very feminine. She did not sit still for a moment. The rope which hung down beside the window to raise and lower the curtain, with its white porcelain weight at the end, fascinated the little animal, and she would jump at it for hours, back and forth, to make it move. She would grab it with her sharp little paws, hang onto it and swing, jump and swing again, without sense and without end. Why did she not prefer to lie quietly in the sunshine? Why did she jump to the cupboard, back to the floor and up again to my desk? She saw me writing, looked mischievously for a moment at my moving pen, and for the next hour she tapped unceasingly against it as if toying with a mouse.

The similarity to the behavior of children is striking. They never walk, but are always on the run. They are always moving around, always busy with something. They can't sit still and, when they are forced to, they cry or kick. Their movement has no real goal; it in itself is their happiness. Later in life the intensity and the rhythm are a bit slowed down, but the pleasure of this kind of doing and acting for its own sake remains. This is the origin of all kinds of sports, and explains, basically, their passionate attraction to millions, although the question of competition introduces important complexities.

Even this narcissistic self-enjoyment can lead, to a certain extent, away from loneliness. It operates as a natural safety valve, an inborn self-regulation which counteracts man's dangerous self-awareness. Thus, activity itself becomes an occupational therapy.

But there is an essential difference between undirected activity on one hand and directed adult activity on the other. The child's movement is still narcissistic; he is seeking self-enjoyment, pure and simple; his movement has no goal outside of itself. The adult, on the other hand, is supposed to have goals, to have attachments and interests outside himself. It is clear, then, that the goal and direction of man's activity are the essential factors in determining whether it can lead him out of his isolation. The cultural aspects of human activity must be properly understood and properly used; narcissistic self-gratifying "social" activity is as regressive and unhealthy as is the narcissistic self-gratification of masturbation.

In all the opportunities society offers for "social" interest, for attachment to causes and individuals outside the self, this danger of narcissism is always present. Man's social leanings are not always the expression of a genuine feeling of empathy, love and partnership, of a need and eagerness to remedy and relieve the sufferings of others. Every so often they are the gestures only of self-indulgence, reflecting the deceiving attitude of a neurotic do-gooder who either tries compulsively to repent for some unconscious guilt feelings or who uses the halo of social virtue as an adornment to hide the enormity of his aggression. Many social workers and nurses, many members and heads of charity organizations, have chosen their professions on the basis of such unconscious motivations. Although they have a distinguished reputation for their driving efficiency, and their memorials are replete with praise for their great character, as proved in their self-sacrificing goodness and devotion, they are essentially hostile, narcissistic personalities.

Such a one was Louise, a stout, commanding woman who had survived the wealthy husband to whom she had been married for twenty-two years. Sitting at his desk, negotiating a big deal with another large company, he had one day simply dropped dead of a sudden heart attack. Louise took his death with what her friends considered admirable fortitude. She made a large contribution to one of her favorite charities in his memory, and, after the appropriate mourning period, threw herself into her ceaseless work for others with renewed zeal. She was known as a great philanthropist: chairman of several civil and charity organizations, trustee and board member of two hospitals. She was an extremely successful fund raiser for all sorts of clubs and agencies—councils for the blind, the underprivileged, the chronically ill. Wherever there was need, one could always rely on Louise's unending zeal and driving power to reach the projected goal. She gave huge sums from her own private fortune—but not before checking into the most minute details of the cases involved. In all her spending there was never a free, spontaneous impulse, never any carefree joy. Every penny and every dollar were recorded and filed and checked and rechecked by her accountant, and her tax returns were the immaculate replicas of her immaculate character.

Louise ruled and commanded the lives of her two children with the same meticulous attention to detail as she displayed in her overwhelming "talent for organization." And she was hard as nails, unbending, power-drunk, ambitious for social prestige, always on the run, driving and being driven.

When I saw her the first time, she was sixty-two and in a period of severe depression. She could not understand the reason for it. More and more frequently she found herself crying "without any sense and reason." Why did the pattern of her life, with all her intense devotion to others, not give her the fulfillment and the feeling of happiness she deserved? She could do what she wanted, she had more than enough money to gratify her most extravagant wishes—although she felt she had none—she was successful, a leading figure in the social life of her community. Then what was it that made her feel so lonely, so unable to enjoy herself?

The clue to this riddle came after a comparatively brief period of her analysis. I had learned that she had had a younger sister whom she "simply adored." This girl had died in childbirth at the age of twenty-eight, after two years of marriage. Louise felt that this sister had always been much "better" than she herself and that she had loved her sincerely.

"Better in what way?"

"Oh, in every way."

"In any specific way you could mention?"

"I really couldn't say. It was just my feeling."

"How did you show your love for her?" I asked.

"I—well, I feel a bit ashamed to say. It sounds like bragging."

"Please, just go ahead, don't feel embarrassed."

"Well, when we were young, my parents didn't have much money. Often the question would come up of which one of the sisters could have a new dress or a new pair of shoes or something. My parents couldn't afford to buy things for both of us at the same time."

"Then you would suggest that your sister should get it instead of yourself?"

"That's it."

"How about schooling? Education?"

"The same. I let her go to college and I took a job. Although I was the more intelligent—at least I think I was."

"I am sure of that."

"Then came the story with Norman."

"Yes?"

She paused. A momentary girlish blush spread over her wrinkled face.

"I was just thinking," she said in a pathetic attempt to hide her feelings, "that he was probably in love with me. And I with him. He was such an unusual guy, he really was."

There was a silence. She had lowered her head. Her lips were trembling slightly.

"I felt that I didn't deserve him—and she was so much better for him, so much more loveable, so much more . . . I know now that I managed to shift his attention and affection to her in a gradual and subtle way. Away from me. First it was a kind of game. Very painful. But probably . . . I think I enjoyed it. And after a while I really didn't care any more—at least I thought I didn't."

"They got married?"

"Yes. They were very happy. For two years. Then she died. In childbirth. Her first child."

Only a few weeks after this session Louise reported a dream. She and her sister were spending a weekend together at a seaside resort. One morning they were on the beach bathing in the surf. A tremendous wave broke right over their heads and almost drowned the sister. It was only at the last moment that she, Louise, was able to pull her out and rescue her.

The interpretation of this dream was as easy as it was enlightening and hardly needed any special associations from the patient. Behind the surface façade of her sacrificing love for her sister, Louise was hiding a murderous hate and unconscious death wish. But her moral censorship was only partly anaesthetized; she made a moral bargain and herself saved the "beloved" sister she wanted to see dead.

During the following hours it became clear that her loathing of this sister sprang from the fact that the parents had shown the younger girl much more affection and attention. All Louise's sacrificing love, all her "social conscience," had been nothing but repeated acts of atonement for her guilt over her unconscious death wishes. This aggression and murderous hate were part of her conventional marriage to her wealthy, but unloved husband. Her guilt remained, and all her social and ethical strivings could not eradicate the aggression, the rage, jealousy and loneliness that lay behind her vaunted "goodness."

Of course, Louise's aggressive do-goodism is not the only kind. The scroll of history is filled with the names of men and women who have been truly devoted to humanity. They—like Florence Nightingale, like Jane Addams—have understood that there can be no genuine interest in the world outside unless there is a genuine awareness of the self. As the infant learns attachment to others through his mother's attachment to him, so he learns respect for himself through her respect for him. The men and women whose childhoods have given them this inside awareness move toward social activity—to charitable, community or political activity—with the same instinctive warmth as they move toward the gratification of their own personal needs. They conquer their loneliness in such activity because they feel it as a part of themselves, rather than as a series of obligations, imposed either by cultural demands or by the demand for atonement of their own hate, guilt and narcissism. Such men and women will not be discouraged from activity by the hypocrisies and parsimonious maneuverings too many contemporary organizations encourage. They will take the Louises in their stride; they are likely to meet many of them. But this will not deter them from expressing their own care for others, by extending their concern to groups and causes which are, in their aspirations if not always in all their personnel, devoted to help for the community. For certainly, genuine involvement in the life of the community is an important weapon in the conquest of loneliness.

Communication between people is, of course, the greatest bridge away from the self. The ability to construct it is characteristic of all normally healthy human beings. This bridge of communication can be thrown across the river of loneliness in many directions. The ones the individual

chooses are functions both of his own interests and character and of the charm the scenery on the mainland holds
for him. The artist makes his work of art a bridge to the
whole of that world. But art is not the only bridge, and the
power necessary to build a link to the outside is within all
men. As the individual adopts a particular religious belief
because of his own background, training and interests, so
he chooses his many bridges to the outside world on this
same basis. What is right for one may not be right for
another; to lay down hard and fast rules as to the objects
towards which one should direct one's energies would be
as wrong as to try to compel the painter to become a writer.

Complex psychological tests are not always necessary to
determine what a person should do. Although they can
help in many situations, usually the individual himself is
aware of the general areas of his interest; nearly every
activity he picks—work, hobbies, community service, or
whatever—will reflect, to some degree, his own personality.
Those whose interests lie in the world of people will show
it not only in their choice of vocation, but of avocation as
well; they are the ones who will derive personal satisfaction from social hobbies and free-time interests. Those who
are more solitary and seclusive, will gravitate towards other
pursuits—reading, music, etc. Yet they will find in these
quiet, impersonal activities as much release from loneliness
as their more outgoing friends find in convivial parties or
meetings.

Yet not everybody consults his own personality in his
choice of activities. Men and women choose their occupations for any number of different motives. One of the most
powerful, alas, is the question of money. An individual
may ultimately accept, for this reason alone, something he
deeply resents; something he has no interest in, no ability

for, and no inclination to do. Other motivations may be social prestige, the halo of artistic saintliness, family pressure or the opposition to it, and finally the desire for naked power. Each time a profession is not an avocation as well, each time a job activity does not correspond with the basic emotional needs or the specific equipment of an individual, a general resentment, restlessness, dissatisfaction, depression and increasing, rather than decreasing loneliness must be expected. The problem might well become complicated in all of those cases where a father demands or at least expects from an only son that he will take over a big industrial enterprise, a store, a profession, etc. Then a severe conflict might open up between true inclinations on the one hand and the feeling of responsibility towards the father on the other.

I remember a young man in his late twenties who preferred to starve in a cold flat, daubing on canvases and hacking at stone, while his wealthy family begged him in vain to become first an apprentice, then a partner and, in the not-too-distant future the vice president of one of the greatest chain stores in the country. The son refused stubbornly to give up his life or accept any money the family was willing to offer him. Only when he found himself involved in a messy situation of blackmail and dangerous publicity did he finally consent, after much prodding and persuasion, to undergo psychiatric treatment. It came just in time to avert a seriously intended suicide. The details of this case, though dramatic, are of no special interest in this context. It is necessary only to say that, when he was given the usual psychological tests, the young man showed great abilities in the very direction his family had wanted him to go. His refusal to accept his family's urgings was motivated by a powerful defense against his unconscious

homosexual dependence on the father. After a comparatively short treatment he decided to join the family firm
and, as I understand, the partnership so far has turned out
to be most successful and satisfying for everybody concerned.

Sometimes routines of work—even of work which offers
no personal satisfactions—are so deeply ingrained that a
job change cannot be made. There are any number of
realistic reasons for this: age, responsibilities, training, to
mention only a few. Not everybody has a job that permits
him to do what he wants to—a job that is meaningful to
him. Social and economic pressures force millions of people into occupations alien to their interests and talents,
but which must be pursued because the individual has to
make enough money to sustain his own life and the lives
of the members of his family. In these cases, his work makes
the individual even more lonely; the impersonality of the
office and the assembly line increases his sense of isolation
and alienation. When the routine, rather than the meaning, of the work becomes the sole content of existence, and
man is forced into overspecialization, he experiences only
some fractional part of the total activity of life. As a cog
in a machine, he knows only his own function. Consequently, his work makes very little sense; it is nothing
but a way to make a living. That is hardly enough and is
bound to cause a loss of perspective.

In these cases, real enjoyment and real fulfillment can
only be found in a hobby. All the time that can be spared
from the hours of forced and lonely toil are given over to
the true vocation, and while four fifths of the week is
squandered on the unloved and unwanted job, devotion is
concentrated and condensed into the precious weekends

and holidays, the tired yet happy leftovers of a lost week.
But even for those whose work is not simply toilsome
drudgery, those who have been fortunate enough to find
in their vocations a meaning that satisfies their own interests, hobbies have important values. At the very least they
provide new stimulations outside of the routine of daily
life. Extending the individual's range of awareness and
concern, they deepen his sense of relatedness to his world.

The solution of the problem of loneliness seems then to
depend to large degree not only upon the role differing
activities play as essential parts of life, but on the degree
to which each of them absorbs the totality of one's existence.
If any one activity becomes the only content of life, if it
envelops the total personality; in other words, if the individual identifies himself with nothing else but this specific
thing, whether accidentally or deliberately chosen, he may
very well lose sight of the other essentials of living. Under
these circumstances, his receiving center is atrophied, his
field of vision is narrowed, he forgets his interval of
existence has to be consciously liked, consumed and fulfilled in all its colors, pleasures, pains and accomplishments.
Perhaps this structure of life will become clearer if it
is thought of in terms of a circle in whose center each man
lives, while the outside world moves around the perimeter.
One can then define in almost mathematical fractions the
kind of life a person lives, the category to which he belongs, by measuring the size of the different sectors. The
narcissistic and in the extreme the psychotic will deny that
perimeter altogether, will deny the reality of the surrounding world. These people live close to their own centers,
with no perimeter at all. They are encased in their un-
breakable loneliness. The compulsive worker, on the other

hand, represents the opposite extreme. All of his being is thrown into and absorbed by the perimeter and his whole life is identified with it. Finally, to follow this mechanical scheme to a graphic representation of a well-balanced life, its structural aspect might be defined as a mixture between the two extremes. A small sector will be taken up by the daily professional life—in the office or laboratory, in a factory or a store. A certain amount of energy, creative or only mechanical, is necessarily consumed here. But something is left for other activities. For hobbies, for community work, for friendships—and for periods of loneliness. The desired proportion and healthy balance can only be reached if the individual bears in mind that the small sector of his professional life is merely a part of his total life, that his existence has other aspects as well. Of course, in order to accomplish something of value, one has to concentrate. In addition, competition has become more and more intense; to get ahead on the social or economic ladder requires an untiring ambition that pushes always forward, toward its goal. There is nothing wrong about this total absorption in a job while it is being done. The danger is that it may become a substitute for the totality of life, instead of being experienced as only an important part of it.

Charles was the youngest in a family of three children. Ten years separated him from his sister, twelve years from his brother. His birth had been unplanned, and not only was he an unexpected arrival, he was unwanted. His parents, meticulous and eminently practical people, had decided even before their marriage they would have only two children: a boy and a girl—no more. For ten years, the husband protected his wife against further pregnancy;

then one day, for some reason, the "protection" failed, and Charles was the consequence.

From his earliest childhood, he was made aware of the fact that he was an "accident." Because the father's guilt was the greater, he was particularly harsh to the boy, and poor Charles grew up as an unwanted intruder in a home that seemed to his child's eyes to consist of four hostile and accusing adults.

He hated himself and was sure that nobody could ever love him, and his whole character developed accordingly. Thrown into his sealed-off loneliness, he became suspicious, withdrawn and compulsively ambitious. He had to make up for the outrage he had done his family and his father in particular; he had to prove to father and to himself that he was a lucky accident.

What followed was a panting, breathless, hectic race to catch up with something he could never win: father's affection. The family was only of moderate income and the guilt-ridden father pointed out at every opportunity that Charles's arrival had reduced their standard of living. Their poverty was Charles's fault; he was an extra mouth to feed, the delivery had been difficult and expensive and it had taken years to pay the additional doctor bills. These constantly reiterated complaints made Charles feel compelled to accept all kinds of menial and insulting after-school jobs. Through the nights he would lie awake in bed studying and reading his school assignments until the gray of the new day. Tired, his head throbbing, he would go to school and then to his dull and boring job. Since he was extremely bright, endowed with a searching intelligence, he passed all his examinations with the highest marks. He threw himself into the academic life of his college with zeal, but did not participate in any of the extracurricular activities. He never went to dances, he avoided girls, he never joined the other boys for bull sessions or for evenings of beer and bravado. He was graduated as valedictorian of his class; he had reached the first plateau in his self-castigating ascent.

Chasing and being chased, Charles eternally held a whip over his own head. He did not enjoy a single hour of his life nor did he know in which specific direction to proceed. He had decided to go into business to prove that he was just as clever as his father. He got a job and every week turned his salary triumphantly over to his greedy parents, who felt that he was doing no more than his duty; he should pay them back for everything they had done for him and everything he had cost them. They began to press him for more money, so Charles went out and looked for a job that would pay a better salary. He gave them everything he made, unable to break away, furious at them and at himself. Now he began to find it difficult to keep a job; he transferred to each of his employers in turn his complex reactions to himself and to his parents. He was convinced that his immense and untiring labors were not sufficiently appreciated, and he quarreled and complained until he was fired. Each dismissal was a new injustice and a new humiliation and bred in him an even more intense need to work still harder.

During all this time he had kept away from women, rationalizing that he had no time for them. He limited his sex activities to masturbation, always accompanied by fantasies of beating and being beaten. One day at work he met a woman several years his senior and of a quite challenging attractiveness. She seduced him and in a short time he married her—or rather, she married him. As one would expect, this legalized bondage served only to feed his sick attachment to the punishing parents whom he despised, loathed and still needed.

For some months the marriage appeared to function fairly well, the sexual roles reversed until the woman began to complain that he did not spend enough time with her, did not care for her and was interested in nothing but his work. Often he stayed at the office until late in the night, and when he did come home early, he spent his evenings on the telephone, discussing with his business associates the complicated deals they never seemed able to consummate during the course of the working day. Slowly this estrangement and the accompanying hate between husband and wife increased. Charles became more and more afraid of a woman whom he had never really loved, and with whom he had never really had a satisfactory sexual relationship, until finally he deteriorated to the point of complete impotence.

At last, a new development occurred. Charles, discouraged and exhausted by his unsuccessful run for recognition and love, realizing with his clear mind the stagnation and growing emptiness of his life, tired of the sterile battles with his wife, of his own hate and disappointment and of the eternal boredom of his meaningless jobs, gave up the fight as lost and retreated back into his childhood loneliness. He had tried his best, and what was the result? Full of bitterness, he began to write, pouring all his suffering and his lonely yearning into verses which, sparked by the flames of his unredeemed sex, at last let out in violent eruptions all the tears he had never cried, all the fear, murder and guilt his wounded mind had kept in lonesome seclusion.

After some hesitation, he sent his work to a publisher, who refused it with a few politely flattering words: "The poems have great quality, but they are too ferocious; I just don't dare to publish them." When he received this reply, Charles only smiled sadly. He should have known; it was fated that he would never succeed. So he went back to the dull routine of a job. In the evenings, after work, he retreated to his studio to write. His wife continued to reproach him more and more bitterly until she began a love affair with a lawyer whom they had met at one of the rare parties she had forced him to attend. Now Charles's defeat seemed complete. Hectic, constantly offended and peeved, he hated himself, the world and the unlucky accident that had brought him into it. He became overefficient, overconscientious, officious, overburdened and unhappy. But he went on working overtime and straining himself mercilessly to do things for which no one ever thanked him. He despised it but he could not stop. The only small pleasure his lonely world ever afforded him came once a month when, in bittersweet resentment, he sent a check to his waiting parents.

This pathetic story, which came to my attention just before it was too late, represents an impressive waste of great human talent and intelligence. Although Charles's near tragedy may be, in its extent, something of an exception, this compulsive slavery, this distortion of the true hope that lies in all work and accomplishment is much too common and can be seen in many different nuances and in varying degrees.

I have observed many men and women who seem finally to have accomplished what they wanted—if any horizon can ever be reached. Those of them who are healthy, feel that at least they are on their way, in their artistic or scientific or technical progress. During their working hours, their absorption is complete and when they finally emerge from behind their desks it takes some time before the veiled expression on their faces gradually disappears and the eyes that seemed blind, focused on something inside themselves, begin to fasten onto outer reality. Stefen Zweig once wrote: *"Nur wer sich ganz verliert, ist sich gegeben."* (Only he who loses himself completely can find himself.) The true meaning of this statement can be understood by comparing life with the changing tides of the ocean: sitting in his small boat, each man has to permit himself to be sucked into the eternal waters. The low tide will always bring him safely back to the land of daily routine. Anchored on the green pasture of his working day, he can let his boat loose into the azure and expose himself in a luminous exultation to the wonder of his lonely life. Then, back again, he will be happy and relaxed, enjoying the morning, the high noon and the stars at night after a day of recklessly absorbing work; a work away from his lonely self.

Whether in a job, in a hobby or in recreation, work is one of the highways to salvation. It became a means of resurrection for a woman who had lost everything when she lost the husband in whom she had invested her whole existence.

Jane had lived with her husband for over twenty years in rare harmony and mutual belonging. When he died, she felt as if it was her own death. After the funeral she refused to see anybody, locked herself in her room and lay down on her bed. She felt the cold numbness of death rising up from her legs, and for days she continued to lie there, sleepless and trembling, on the bed where now she was suddenly alone and petrified. The old familiar objects they had lovingly bought and collected were still around her: the books they had discussed through many precious hours, the furniture they had found, with the pride of explorers, in quaint antique shops—all those small things that seem insignificant and that yet make up the essence of life in common until everything is over. Each of them is linked to a memory, to a specific hour. The hardest thing to bear, somehow, was his clothing: the shirts and socks and underwear, everything she had bought for him, all the gifts of her love; all the personal things he had worn on the beloved body that was now lying somewhere cold under the earth, no more to be tended or caressed. And here she was, lying on her bed. His hand no longer held hers when she could not sleep because she was worrying about some trifle that now seemed to have been so unimportant. All the tiny gestures, the inflection of his dark voice—kind or angry, yet always beloved—all that was gone forever and nothing was left but this stillness and her own lonesome breathing: this horrible loneliness, unbearable, eternal. Through the endless hours of the night she thought of killing herself. The telephone rang until finally it stopped. The air was stiff and cold; there was complete emptiness. She did not need to destroy herself, this was death already.

Later on she could not remember how long she had lain there like that. The hours, the time crept on. She remembered vaguely that the shadows grew darker in the evening and that the hopeless gray of another dawn tried in vain each morning to filter through the drawn curtains. Then, one day, one hour, no different from the others, she decided to get up. She went over to the mirror on the bureau. She stared at the red, swollen face, the untidy gown, the disheveled hair. Automatically, she began to comb her hair and to powder her nose. It took her a long time. Then she got dressed. She put on the simple blue woolen coat he had always liked best. For a moment the wound and the deep soreness under her ribs came back. She felt dizzy and had to lie down on the bed. Two minutes later she felt better and forced herself to get up. She went to the phone. She called one of her elderly friends, a woman who had tried unsuccessfully to reach her, calling hourly through all these days. They had lunch together. She tried to swallow the food, but she could not keep it down.

In the evening she felt quieter, and for the first time since his death she slept soundly; her friend had finally persuaded her to take a sleeping pill. Gradually life came back to her. She began to eat regularly, to answer the letters that had piled up. She got in touch with her lawyer and settled up her husband's affairs. Every few hours the dull pain of her loneliness came back in excruciating spells that threw her into hopeless despair. She knew that she had to make up her mind either to "end it all" or to get to work, to find a new sense for her wrecked life. She decided on the second alternative.

She bought a house in one of New York's suburbs—a small, cheerful house with a steep gable and a huge garden, and began to take care of children—children whose parents were divorced or were going away for a few weeks' vacation or who did not know how to handle their sons and daughters because they did not realize that the children's "bad" behavior and violence were only the echoes of their own disturbances.

Jane took care of all of them with the intensity and warmth that her lonesome heart could give them. She worked with them through the days and cared for them at night when they could not sleep, or were sick, or felt their own loneliness as a result of the separation from their parents. She taught them to read and to write and answered, as well as she could, all the endless questions children ask. She told them the names of the flowers in the garden, explained how they grew and how they had to be watered, what diseases they might develop. She described the countries from which they had come. In the evenings she played with them or read to them; the smile on her face seemed to prove her inner security and peace. The pangs of her loneliness came less often and were less severe, and she gave herself to her work without restraint.

The most moving events were the great holidays, such as Christmas. For this occasion she would prepare for days, hanging the bright room with brighter pictures the children had painted, buying the tallest tree and hanging all kinds of wonders on its feathery green branches: stars and silver chains and candles. She disappeared for long, mysterious hours, buying everything children enjoy, intuitively knowing what each child liked best. When finally the great day arrived, she put on her best dress and saw to it that each child, too, was dressed with special care. Then she lined them up in a semicircle and sat down in the middle, and, after a gramophone played first a Bach cantata and then some carols, she would read, with a trembling voice, the story of the birth of the Redeemer who had come down from heaven to earth so that no one should ever be alone, but should always be loved and protected under His great cloak. Changing the old Biblical story a bit here and there, she gave her own version of the great happiness she had to tell. As she sat bent to read from the book that lay in her lap, she looked like one of the sibyls or prophets of the Sistine Chapel, broad, firm and with an expression of visionary bliss.

The days went by. The children who had refused to eat when they were at home with their parents gained weight and their pale cheeks became pink and round. The destructive ones learned to acknowledge the fact that the other children had the same rights and the same little sufferings as they, and these had to be respected. The flowers blossomed in spring and died with the winter. One season followed another, and the life that had been on the brink of lonely collapse found its sense and goal by working hard and relentlessly for the happiness of these children.

When Jane had bought the house and the garden, there had been nothing around but green lawns, trees and bushes. Then a new highway was built, which cut through the unspoiled land, and soon the bulldozers began to level down the sprouting life. Cement and steel took the place of the serene and dreaming country, and in no time houses stood there, red, rectangular, and ugly, one looking just like the other, practical, hygienic, with neither charm nor beauty. The stillness was gone, stores were served by rumbling trucks, and in one year this hurrying, restless clamor had recklessly destroyed the lovely face of the earth. The day came when, already surrounded on three sides by those modern cave dwellers, the dead windows of whose houses stared blindly at her tiny flower island, Jane was offered a high price to give up her home, her garden and her children because the grounds were needed for another of those naked six-story houses. Bravely she refused. Who would take care of the children? This was her life, her work and devoted duty; here in this garden of blooming flowers she had replanted her own life and had found her new happiness, and no money could tempt her to give it up.

The struggle was on. Since it soon became obvious that the stubborn "old maid" would not sell for any price, the hyenas around her began to howl. They tried to ruin her

reputation by spreading false reports: she was cruel to the
children and beat them. When that device failed—because
the children's parents realized the obvious health and happiness of their youngsters—the hyenas changed their methods. They reported to the city health department and to
the fire department that Jane's house was not safe, that it
was a fire hazard; they spread rumors in the religious community that she was an agnostic; they whispered that she
did not have a degree and was not qualified to run such a
place; that the children were sick. They made much of the
fact that she was not American-born and hinted that there
was some dark secret in her past. She stood it all with firm
serenity, although her face began to grow a bit paler and
a fine line appeared, cutting from the bridge of her nose up
through her forehead. Nor was her gait as firm as before. A
light stoop of her shoulders became visible. Still, she sat
up many nights with a coughing child, and would get up
time and time again to comfort him, even though her feet
were swollen and her breathing had become a bit heavy.

The last thing she fought through triumphantly was a
court summons given out by an unscrupulous lawyer who
would have done anything that had the smell of money
about it. The cellar of the house next door was eight feet
lower than hers, and Jane was ordered to build a high fence
around her plot for safety's sake. One morning a letter
arrived with the news that the neighbor was willing to pay
the bulk of the cost of construction. Jane, elated, walked
over to the place in question together with one of the children, who had begged her to show him the interesting
"abyss." When the little boy, eager and full of excitement,
slipped, she grabbed him and pulled him back just as he
was falling. In saving him from certain injury, she lost her

own balance and tumbled the length of the embankment into the stony courtyard.

She did not regain consciousness before she died. The children and the neighborhood were stunned. Hundreds of people flocked to her funeral; full of grief they stared into the open casket where she lay, dressed in a simple white gown, still and peaceful, her lips formed in a strange and almost frightening smile. In the last moments before her breathing stopped, the knowledge must have slipped through her beclouded mind that her life had not been wasted; that she was not alone; that she had given much to those children and helped them grow into happy adults; and that all these people, parents and children alike, would never forget what she had done for them.

Here ends the story of this remarkable woman who conquered her loneliness by courageously going to work. Still, all her doing would have gone down in a sterile void unless it was blended into the one greatest gift: a unique and all-embracing warmth.

✻

CHAPTER NINE

Of Sex, Love and Redemption

ALL ROADS LEAD to Rome, the ancients said. They re-
ferred not only to the actual network of Roman highways
but, on a sublimated level, to the spiritual quality and way
of life embodied in the Roman Empire: order, power, decency, the law, political and economic organization—a
civilization which in its best days produced a cultural level
that benefited the whole of mankind. But the roads no
longer lead to Rome; the Empire fell and on its ashes a
Christian civilization was built, which for two millennia
has declared love to be the universal center and goal as well
as the sole pathway to redemption. Although the Western
world has subscribed to this credo, has adopted it as an
official way of life, practically no one follows it, and the
ferocious instincts of hate and murder in all their manifold
and dangerous disguises make a mockery of this design for
living.

Why has this happened? Why have two thousand years
of fierce struggle not brought humanity closer to an ideal
it has accepted theoretically as mankind's greatest satisfaction? The answer is simple. The old instinctual drives, the
old heritage of the beasts, still live in all their strength in
everybody, and the higher, controlling centers of the brain
still battle in vain for a final supremacy over the ugly legacy
from the past. If one wants to know something about hu-

man nature, one has only to look at the Ten Commandments. Man does not have to be ordered to do what is in accordance with his nature; each one of the Commandments, as a moral demand, opposes all the deeper drives that man still hugs to himself, still refuses to give up. One day he will have to, or he will die of loneliness or in mutual destruction.

What is this phenomenon of love to which man has theoretically dedicated himself and which in actuality he finds so hard to attain? To evaluate it in its true significance, it has first to be washed and dry-cleaned. All its common patina of sweetness, sentimentality and abusing sanctimoniousness must be scoured off. Like the word "loneliness" it has fallen into a kind of intellectual disrepute and one always feels a bit embarrassed in speaking about it. Why has this happened? This pet of the writers, artists, philosophers, film producers and every petit bourgeois alike has been psychiatry's stepchild. Is this neglect only the psychiatrist's unconscious defense against the same embarrassment that makes film audiences respond with sniggers to scenes of more or less tasteful love-making on the screen? Or is it simply a confusion derived from Freud's rather unfortunate coining of the word "libido," to describe the sex drive in all of its ramifications?

The very use of the expression "love-making" puts one in the middle of a semantic thicket, equating love and sex. To define love, then, one must first cut away the underbrush of sex in order to see what is left. Evidently, "making love" has little to do with love but deals rather with a sexual play consciously directed towards seduction—a play that can be carried on either with or without love. Because Sex is not Love.

As a matter of fact, aggression and hate—love's direct

antitheses—are to some extent parts of sex. Destructive rather than creative elements are at the root of man's drive to overpower his woman. When this hatred trespasses beyond a certain threshold and appears in the unconscious as murderous drives—a situation the psychiatrist sees in so many of his neurotic patients—sexual potency is thwarted. But the question remains: are the guilt and the hate nothing but the results of infantile frustrations transferred into adult life so that the sex partner is experienced as and unconsciously identified with a forbidding or domineering parent, is the hate only a projected fight against one's own dependence? Or is this phenomenon generally characteristic of the species Homo sapiens? Is the drive to overpower a given individual in a specific situation identical with a general drive for mastery and self-assertion—that is, with aggression? If this were true, sex would be akin to a common human impulse to possess and incorporate, together with a narcissistic craving for relief of tension, so that the partner is only used—or rather misused—as a pawn for self-gratification.

"What has going to bed with a man got to do with anything?" a patient once pounded at me indignantly. "You're just an old-fashioned moralist." And another muttered: "I only slept with him on and off to get rid of him."

A man described his fantasy naïvely and with no intended cynicism: he was lying in bed alongside a girl and contentedly smoking his cigarette, while his penis shot over to her and had intercourse with her. To be sure, this patient was paranoid, a psychotic; still anybody might detach himself from the sexual act, out of guilt and hate.

"There is no contact between me and my husband," a neurotic and, of course, frigid woman once said of her marital life, "except that we are both naked." Here is a perfect description of complete isolation. This woman was unable to build the bridge from the I to the You because her unconscious hate of her husband, of any man, made it impossible for her to give herself. When she was a young child, her brother, who was the parents' preferred child, getting all their love and affection while his sister remained starved and lonesome, raped her. The combination of parental rejection and the experience with her brother inevitably distorted her pattern of response. It seemed to her that it was necessary to be a boy in order to be loved, as her brother was. If she was a boy she would possess the bodily instrument through which she could revenge her disappointment and her aggressive hate. How could she, armed with such a fantasy of being a man herself, "give herself" to another man who, with each intercourse, wounded and hurt her?

Thus it becomes evident that hate is the mainspring of our loneliness, the enemy number one. It is hate that makes it impossible for the individual to build the bridge to the other. The only thing we have to hate—to paraphrase a famous statement—is hate itself. Again and again I have been appalled to see what this destructive drive does to human beings by its ferocity, by its senseless, pathetic and sterile waste of energies, by the way it keeps the individual away from the one thing that makes life livable and valuable: love. "When you take my hate away, what am I supposed to live on?" a young woman once screamed at me, jumping up furiously from the couch and staring at me with her hard, icy-blue eyes. She hated her husband, her children, her parents, her analyst and, of course, most profoundly herself. She was unable to imagine any other bondage but hate. How could she give it up? If she did, nothing would be left of her but her own hateful and lonesome being.

Hate is not the only obstruction. There is another: anxiety, the fear of being "owned," a fear which is the transference and projection into adult life of the child's relationship to his mother and his dependence on her. The result, as far as men are concerned, is a sexual reaction not unlike that of the psychotic described earlier: a kind of sexual relation without real object attachment; in psychological terms no different from masturbation. There is no relationship at all to the other human being; the woman's sexual organ is used only to provide a narcissistic release of tension.

"I compartmentalize my love," a young woman explained once in sad cynicism. "During the day I am narcissistic, and in the evening, when 'papa' comes home from his office, I love." Love? Love cannot be turned off and on like an electric light switch. Sex and love often seem to be conceived of either as a kind of exciting sport or as a hygienic game. Because sex is not the same as love, it does not function well under these circumstances. Although the "modern" approach sees sex as "liberation," few people seem to be able to find release in its pursuit. Each of the partners in the sex act remains encapsulated in his own loneliness.

Such disturbed sexual reactions in women lead to frigidity, shockingly prevalent, especially in this country. I remember the typical report of a young, attractive, unmarried woman who met a man and spent a day with him in the harmony of mutual enjoyment: they swam, sunbathed, ate together, had a stimulating conversation, they laughed and they kissed. The evening arrived, "and now," to quote her, "the misery begins."

What produces this cold misery? How can it be understood and explained? What blocks the road to a real linkage of individuals; what prevents men and women from building that desired and longed-for bridge between two people, so that each can break free from his lonely isolation? Why in so many cases cannot man solve this most vital and intrinsic problem of life?

In relation to our own country, one might suggest first an historical explanation. It is not too long ago that the early settlers had to fight for their lives. The women had to be sturdy and strong and masculine; every so often they had to take over the men's jobs in order to survive. Their femininity had to be put on ice. They were good companions, courageous, brave, hard and helpful. And they were good competitors, too. When the land itself was finally conquered, a sociological situation developed which intensified the pattern the problems of the pioneers had produced. With the beginning of the machine age and the emancipation of women, they began to stream into industry and to become part of the labor force, competing with men for jobs that had heretofore been exclusively masculine property. Two world wars sent the men away in uniform, thus decimating the labor force and accelerating this process. But there were other, even more significant reasons for this dangerous development.

The establishment of the factory and the office forced men to leave their women for more than half the day. When they came home, tired from the day's work and often unable to clear their minds of the fog of that atmosphere, they were called upon by their wives or sweethearts for entertainment, sexual or otherwise. And frequently, because the men were physically and mentally exhausted, they could not live up to these demands. The real masculinity their culture had imposed on women was now exaggerated in the minds of men, who began to see women only as devouring and insatiable. Thus the sexes began to run away from one another, and homosexuality, male and female, latent and overt, conscious and unconscious, developed to a perilous peak. Today the women get together to play mah-jongg or other games while the men prefer to spend their hours of "overtime" in bars in the company of alcohol and other men.

The significance of this sociological development seems to be largely unrecognized. It presents a major barrier to the conquest of loneliness. Involved here is not only the question of the alarming amount of sexual impotence in men and women but even more the question of a disturbed conditioning and training for normal sexual functioning, a disturbance in the ability to love. For this involves flexibility of the personality—or the ability to change its dynamic balance.

It would be ridiculous to raise an accusing finger at this or that individual; the problem is not one of judgment but of diagnosis and cure. Nevertheless, the fact is that many American women—more than their European sisters—have not developed emotionally far enough past the narcissistic state of infancy. The perennial and vulgar advertising of a cult of cold beauty, whose ideal is uniformity and success, has already reaped its poisonous fruits. So many American women are neither ready nor willing to give themselves to their men, to submit, to let go. Instead, they remain cold and narcissistic, and want only to be admired. In many cases it appears that they are concerned only to conquer the man and then to refuse him. In this sense, intercourse is for them a means of deflating the man, and they enjoy it to the degree to which they experience this dubious pleasure. The wrong scale of values they have embraced, the false evaluation of pride into which they have been trapped—these do not permit relationships of real meaning or value to develop. This envy of the man, this competition with him, this wish to dominate him, blinds them to the fact that *a woman's weakness is her strength,* and that only a sick man—a latent or overt homosexual— desires a "strong" that is, a masculine woman.

Of course, this does not in any way excuse the men, who are clumsy lovers, who do not know that women want more than to be penetrated in intercourse; that they want to be caressed and fondled; that they want and need attention, delicacy of affection, in short, love; that the physiological act of intercourse in itself is not, for many women, the important goal at all. The American man does not understand that the sex curve is different in men and women; that it takes a woman longer to get excited because she is embedded more deeply in her loneliness; and that it takes her longer to get out of her excitement once it has been aroused. In addition, his fear and hate of dominating women often blinds him to the real values in femininity and makes him antagonistic to them. He is contemptuous of woman's sensitivity, her mood-swing; he is so conditioned that he becomes suspicious and afraid if she is willing to assume a truly feminine role in the relationship. The overbearing woman and the defeated man produce their duplicates as their offspring, and the vicious circle by which each of the sexes moves further away from its own nature and fulfillment becomes ever more difficult to escape.

The sexes are certainly equal; economic, social, political, or intellectual discrimination against either is positively wrong. But equality does not mean identity. The biological differences between men and women have their counterparts in psychological differences. When either sex tries to compete with the other and take over its characteristics, difficulties will inevitably arise. The more "masculine" the women become, and the more "feminine" the men, the harder it is for each to build the bridge to the other. A bridge does not link two particles which are indistinguishable from one another; it links two separate, distinct and different entities. Each needs the bridge to gain from the other that which he cannot supply himself. Why bother to construct it in the first place if it does not lead to something different from the self?

If, in trying to understand the psychodynamics of love, one again thinks in terms of the relationship and proportion among ego, id and superego, one will find that in a love situation, the ego and the moral censorship of the superego lose their dominant position; there is a partial temporary blackout in their functioning, and the id takes over in almost unlimited expansion. Lovers experience this changing feeling of themselves with wondering fascination. It seems as if something has happened to them that they neither wanted nor directed; as if an alien power which they cannot identify with themselves has taken possession of them. As happens so often, language unconsciously reveals the deeper layers of this strange process in a precise and perfect fashion. One speaks of "falling" in love, a phrase that expresses vividly the fact that the ego topples down from its throne, and finds itself suddenly confused and powerless, controlled completely by the instinctual heritage of the id. And this is accompanied by a collapse of one of the most precious accomplishments of human evolution: the sense of reality judgment.

Lovers, notwithstanding the degree of their usual capacity to grasp reality, seem to undergo an increasing blurring and deterioration of their ability to judge the surrounding world, especially the qualities of their love object and everything connected with it. This astonishing extinction of intellectual capacities and qualities which did exist before is due to an idealization of and a more or less complete identification with the love object. The ugliest faces become angelic, moral turpitude is perceived as an excess of virtue. The process of idealization reaches a climax of reality distortion and irrationality.

Extraordinary as are the alterations in the function of the ego, the changes in the operation of the moral censorship are even more impressive. The most restrained individuals become uninhibited and daring; they are willing to meet any challenge as long as it will benefit their beloved. No sacrifice is too great, and even the most powerful of all instincts—the instinct of self-preservation—may be given up with a happy smile. The lover who is willing to commit any crime as long as it will please his beloved, is equally willing to murder her at the moment his own emotional gratifications are stopped. The newspapers daily provide examples of such occurrences—both of love's heroism and its cruelty. All this is related to two other spectacular manifestations of disturbed emotional balance: heightened possessiveness and generally increased instability of the total personality.

The all-embracing possessiveness derives its intensity from identification with the idealized love object. Such a feeling of complete oneness has best been expressed in Plato's Eros. In this symbolic legend, Plato describes human beings as having originally had four legs, four arms, two noses, two mouths, etc. Because they did evil, the gods decided to punish them by cutting each individual in two. The skin was roughly sewn together over the wound—the navel remains to represent the eternal scar and memory of this tragic event—and in the whirlwind that followed, the two halves of each individual became separated and lost one another. Ever since then, says Plato, they long to be reunited. This longing is what we call Eros, or love.

The story fails to explain what its author wanted it to—the mysterious phenomenon of infatuation. But it does describe, in poetic symbolism, the intensity of belonging that lovers feel—the phenomenon science calls identification.

For it is identification that explains the violence of jealousy a lover experiences when he feels threatened—in actuality or only in his imagination—with the loss of his love object. This loss means to him—as Othello's rage, murder and suicide dramatically show—that he will be reexposed to his loneliness, to the deadly anxiety of being forced to face the world and its threatening and confusing strangeness alone. No Tristan dares to live without his Isolde, no Romeo without his Juliet. Life would be without sense, an eternal and hopeless struggle. "Love is the fear of being alone," the novelist Storm once said. The statement could be rephrased in more scientific terms: love is a defense against the anxiety of loneliness.

To watch attentively the peaceful bliss on the faces of two lovers—who stare into each other's eyes for many minutes in complete silence and oblivion of everything that is going on around them—is to grasp the astonishing experience of the "double," the reflection of one's self in another, or rather, the reflection of one's needed complement. This seems to reveal the narcissistic nature of passion: the emotion becomes nothing but a means of gratification, a way of receiving the rays of one's own image reflected in a mirror.

Freud felt that the desired love partner is merely a projection of the mother, and the happiness and rapture of love nothing but a return to the womb. Although its simplicity and neatness make such a hypothesis tempting, it illuminates the dangerous trap into which even a critical genius like Freud can fall when he tries to squeeze everything into one formula, even if that formula has proved to be of basic importance in many human relationships. Freud's keen sense of clinical observation is certainly indicated by this proposal; the psychiatrist sees in his practice many love partners who are picked after the shape, personality, profession, interests and general pattern of the parent, and this is especially evident in those cases in which the choice has fallen on a much older person. But one must doubt that this is a general rule; rather, it seems to be a pathological sign common among neurotics, and this may be the explanation for Freud's dubious reasoning. Loneliness, anxiety and the protection against them may well be the driving instinctual power behind the phenomenon of love. But why limit its purpose exclusively to a return to the mother image? I would like instead to suggest a much broader approach to the whole phenomenon which, while not neglecting the importance of the longing for the mother image, assigns this yearning a symbolic rather than a realistic meaning.

The psychiatrist has learned to look upon the dynamics behind emotional disease as a kind of regression—regression on an individual, ontogenetic basis. Such regression is either a neurosis or a psychosis, depending on the degree of its severity. This retreat creates a change in the individual's entire emotional economy. The severity of the disease is measured by the extent of that change; by the degree to which the ego-functions are given up, that is, the degree to which the conscious directing center loses its dominant position. In psychosis, the ego boundaries are absolutely transgressed and the individual experiences himself as does the newborn baby: he is at one with everything, he no longer experiences himself as an individual. In neurosis, the retreat is only relative and less severe.

The similarity between the behavior of neurotic and psychotic individuals on the one hand and lovers on the other is striking. Everybody has experienced or noted the playful silliness of lovers, their baby talk, their violent mood-swings; a behavior that displays more than a coincidental similarity to and imitation of childhood manners. If one adds to this the self-forgetting, vacuous stare, the absurd smile strangely reminiscent of the self-contained look of many psychotics, one might suspect that behind the phenomenon of passionate love the same regressive mechanism operates as in the case of those sick people, the only difference being that in the case of the lover, the process is not individual, not ontogenetic, but phylogenetic. It appears that the lover is returning not to an earlier period in his own personal development, but to an earlier period in the development of the race itself.

If this is true, one would suspect that love itself represents a defense reaction against the evolutionary development of the human race, which has brought man from the non-conscious forms of animal life to the unbearable self-awareness, the anxious feeling of loneliness, associated with his most recently developed evolutionary acquisition: his cortex. In giving up this structure, man goes back to a happy, subcortical, thalamic existence; returns to that dreamlike world of Eden from which God expelled him in order that he should grow into Man. Apparently, such an abandonment of his most precious possession—the thinking part of his brain—is to the human race the only way to avoid the terror of loneliness.

One difficulty, however, emerges in such a definition of love: the phenomenon of love in animals, the tender relationship of dogs to their masters, or an apparent love relationship between male and female animals of the same species seems to contradict such an hypothesis. Are the animal and human phenomenon the same? On the basis of observation, it seems that the similarity is only a surface one.

What then are the differences? Experience bears out the fact that in the case of animals, one deals merely with a kind of conditioned reflex, whereas the irrationality of both its existence and its development is one of the intrinsic qualities of human passion. A man, surrounded by hundreds of women, may ignore all of them save one—the one he desires, while the animal will "love" any master or mistress who gives him food and shelter.

As far as the mutual love of animals is concerned, I do not think that this should be confused with its human counterpart, either. Animals rarely maintain one love object over a long period of time; in the few cases where such an attitude actually seems to exist, it is obviously based entirely on a sexual predilection and affinity.

Several clinically observed experiences seem to prove the validity of the theoretical conception advanced here. First, it gives a clear understanding of the behavior of the neurotic who is afraid to love. If passion means the transgression of the ego-boundaries, it becomes evident that the neurotic, whose ego is weak and threatened, cannot afford to "give himself up," but is forced to cling desperately to the "I" he has. Of course, one must admit that this fear of

losing himself may not be the only reason for his inability
to love; in addition, there is always his hatred.

Still, one does not necessarily have to deal with the
pathological behavior of the neurotic to grasp the significance of this hypothesis. For it seems to throw light on
a common experience of the normal individual in our
culture, who finds that marriage produces emotional
changes in his relationship to his beloved. While the
dreamy premarital love relationship vibrates in an atmosphere of irrationality, the rhythm of married life, its sober
and continuous pressure of daily routine, the demands and
needs of a family, the rigid steel frame of professional and
social order, make it impossible for the individual to shut
himself off forever from reason and reality. Gradually, the
absolute reign of the thalamus is given up and the primacy
of the cortex is restored. Husband and wife undergo an
evolutionary growing-up process. Thus one witnesses a
gradual change in the emotional temperature between
marriage partners. Slowly, the passionate, compulsive and
psychotic heat of the regression subsides. Following it and
in its place develops a mutual feeling of profound security
and human warmth. This abundant pleasure of rational
understanding more than compensates for its loss of color.
In marriage the bridge trembles every so often. It is
shaken under the impact of unavoidable storms of disagree-
ment: disagreements on money, on the education of the
children, on attitudes towards friends, books, movies or
politics. But this bridge must never break.

For the benign psychosis of love is the main support over
the black river of loneliness. It demands that the individual give up infantile narcissism and shift his concerns
from himself towards an object in the outside world. In the
normal course of development, this object will be a person

of the opposite sex. All thoughts and inner forces, the totality of the individual's emotional existence, are slowly geared towards and involved in the happiness, the smile and the well-being of the beloved person. This smile is more important than all his own tears; his self-pity, his complaints disappear under the warmth of this feeling; and his care, his tenderness, his stormy wish to help become more meaningful because they are directed towards someone else.

It may be that our whole system of ethical values and demands is dictated not only by social necessity, but by the individual's need for protection against that evolutionary development that has taken the human race far out into the open sea of terrifying isolation. The regression to love may have all the earmarks and symptoms of a disease—a psychosis. But it is a benign psychosis, the only one we do not intend to cure.

Life, as an eternal question mark of sense and value, is then answered in terms of temperature. The icy wind of loneliness hisses over the frozen face of humanity, threatening to extinguish life as surely as the Ice Age extinguished whole animal species. The hot wind of passion and infatuation, mingled with the cold, produces the only temperature in which man can thrive—the climate of love.

For reality is not enough. Though one of psychiatry's main tasks is to break and dissolve the disturbing and often paralyzing effects of magical thinking, nevertheless man does not live by bread alone. He has a need for the irrational. Time and again I have watched with dismay the often dangerous side effects of psychoanalytic treatment: after a so-called successful analysis, the former patient begins to "analyze" everything and everybody including himself. Obviously, his own analysis is not really finished

because he is using his newly acquired knowledge primarily as a tool to inflate his still-weak ego. Instead of
experiencing a rich, colorful existence, he reduces all of
life to the white and dry skeleton of psychology. He may
derive from this the poor gratification of an intellectual
accomplishment, but at the same time he impoverishes the
richness and abundance of life itself. It seems to be of intrinsic importance to successful living that the miracle of
this life should stay in each individual as an undercurrent of his hourly experience. "Understanding" everything might sometimes very well be equal to losing the
core of it.

On the other hand, man does not live by cake alone
either. He cannot subsist on a cheap, amorphous mysticism,
immersed in the slimy waters of sentimental sweetness.
This leads only to a distasteful and pathetic escape.

Reality—which in some way might be only a mirage itself
—must by no means be evaded; it has only to be imbibed
with wonder, lived as a part of the canvas of man's total
existence.

The meaning of each man's life depends less on what he
does than on the warmth he is able to radiate. This most
personal, most intimate warmth is the only salvation. It is
this love that makes bearable the life into which he is
born, helpless, with all the others around him. They, like
him, are born, breathe, love, hate and fight, and after a
brief time, the whole show is over. Everyone sits on this
small bench holding hands. Because behind, in the dark
corner, waits the shapeless and frightening shadow of death.

Few have grasped the key experience of life: he who
gives more, gets more. This fact is neither a piece of sticky
sentimentality nor a back-slapping Babbittry. It is a straight
statement of the law of experience. Although it may seem

paradoxical in a materialist frame of thought, it is nevertheless a true expression of the verities of emotional and
spiritual existence. Because when one throws a bridge
over the river, the other will come walking towards him,
unfailingly and grateful that he has been summoned.

This is where sex comes in—not the other way around.
One cannot begin with the end. The man or woman who
walks out of his door looking for sexual adventure will
easily find a partner who, after the usual ascent through a
movie, a meal, a dance and a few drinks at a bar, will provide the desired "pleasure." But after the event, both will
be left with disgust and nothingness. Sex can be easily,
quickly and impatiently consumed. Love takes time. It
has to grow and unfold slowly—like everything that is a
part of life. It takes time to break the boundaries of loneliness. Man is too tightly kept in and by himself and, aside
from the few exceptions in which love hits like lightning,
the tiny spark sprouts over weeks and months and sometimes years until suddenly the flame springs up to illu-
minate all of life. Then the other is wanted, his whole
being is desired; the lover wants to be in him, bodily and
mentally and emotionally. And again language expresses
the unconscious more clearly: men and women "give"
themselves in love, find their deliverance in surrender.

Once I was called upon to treat a man who literally
could not pass over bridges. This was his main symptom,
frightening and disturbing indeed to one who had to travel
a great deal. He was extremely bright, but he could not
conceive what might be the cause of this alarming symptom. He did not realize that bridges had for him the same
unconscious meaning and symbolic significance they have
for everyone: the link between people. Something, then,
must have occurred in the life of this man that blocked the

construction of the link, or, rather, that had blocked his own desire toward some person with whom he could not permit himself to be joined. This person, it developed, was his mother, about whom as a child he had felt so guilty and hostile that he had to block the bridge each time he wanted to pass over it. He hated her and loved her and he had to punish himself for this murderous hate by the fantasy that he would fall off the bridge into the deep waters and drown.

The bridge is always there, always waiting. Those who put up the barriers themselves, for reasons of their own unconscious choice, will remain their own prisoners, never taking that step that leads out of loneliness to the other side of life. This bridge does not lead necessarily only to another person—although this is the deepest and most redeeming experience. It might lead to any object in the outside world, or to the whole of it, to an identification with every other being, with its wishes, its sufferings, its pain and its happiness. This is the love to which the Judeo-Christian ethic aspires. It demands active help, active care. It will remain nothing but a sterile duty as long as it is not recognized as the greatest road away from loneliness.

Among the most venerable and most beloved of all the saints is Saint Francis of Assisi. It is not so much that he cast off his lavish clothes, the luxuries of rich food, housing and money; not so much that, clad in a simple garment, he voluntarily took up the life of the poor. It is less the utter simplicity of his life than his teaching; the lesson of a humble and universal love—a love of flowers, of trees, birds and all men and all animals alike. It is this simplicity, this unsentimental integrity, it is this genuineness—this gesture of bending down lovingly to the smallest speck of life around him—that endears him.

When one drives up the hill on which the village and the famous two-story church of Assisi are located, one feels the serenity and dreamlike beauty of the landscape, this simple portion of earth over which the saint walked, living the great message he gave to the world. The last rays of the evening sun glimmer in silvery shafts through the violet shadows of the streets, and the faint breeze barely touches the deep peace of the church. No place on earth seems, in its moving simplicity, to be more the embodiment of man's oldest yearning: to be at one with his surrounding world.

A few weeks ago, while walking through Central Park, I was reminded of the atmosphere and intrinsic meaning of the Italian town. It had just stopped raining, and in the mist I could see an old man bending down to a sparrow. For a moment it seemed as if the two were conversing. The old man's beard was ragged and unkempt. He wore shabby clothes and high rubber boots; his entire appearance was that of those queer, disturbed and lonely persons one occasionally sees feeding the squirrels and pigeons. All these people have something pitiful and a bit grotesque in their bearing; one passes them with a shrug and then forgets about them the next minute. Here, however, something seemed different. This man's whole body was bent so deeply that his old head almost touched the earth. There was a strange smile on his wrinkled face and the humble gesture made him seem like a modern Saint Francis. A little boy of about eight stood a few feet away from him. He was dressed in a cowboy suit, a pistol in his broad leather belt. He had been taught to shoot and hate and kill in a playful way, as many youngsters are, through the cheap and false romanticism of the movies and similar "educational" agencies. He was well and neatly dressed, obviously the son of well-to-do parents who lived comfortably in one of the apartment houses that line the park. His hand on his pistol, he debated for a moment whether or not to shoot at the man. Something made him change his impulse and he stood there, silent and a bit tense, until finally he walked towards the stranger, slowly and shyly, step by step, standing close to the man and finally bending down beside him. After a few seconds, the bird fluttered away. It began to rain again and the last I could make out through the fine drizzle was the picture of the two standing together involved in a long conversation; a conversation that will throw its influence into the boy's future, into his adult life.

Love, in the final analysis, is an attitude, a general approach to the world that surrounds us. Not only to a single person, but to objects, to nature, to any creation of the universe. It reflects the development from a social empathy to an emotional state in which the demand "Love thy neighbor as thyself" has become the generalized formula for redemption. It asks for the abandonment of primitive hate, murder and aggression, and promises as a reward the suspension of anxiety, loneliness and isolation.

If man can raise the glassy curtain that separates him from the rest of the world from the moment of his birth, he will fill the empty seat beside him with his own life. With love, he can transform this world into his own kingdom, so that the frontiers finally vanish into nought, and the barriers melt away.

ABOUT THE AUTHOR

Eric P. Mosse's life runs in two distinguished parallel lines: literary and psychiatric. They are fused for the first time in this book.

A member of the family that once owned one of the most influential European newspaper trusts, Dr. Mosse studied medicine at the universities of Freiburg, Koenigsberg, Berne, Berlin and Munich. He was associated with hospitals in Munich and Berlin and studied at the Berlin Psychoanalytic Institute. In addition to becoming a successful psychoanalyst, he found time to write four novels, several plays and numerous short stories, articles and essays. He was active as a director of plays and as literary adviser to a theatrical trust that at one time controlled seven of Berlin's leading theatres.

Dr. Mosse came to this country in the early nineteen thirties. He has served on the psychiatric staffs of Mount Sinai and Bellevue hospitals, New York University Medical School and the New York State Psychiatric Institute. He has been a guest lecturer at the New School for Social Research and has addressed many psychological societies at Brooklyn College, C.C.N.Y. and Hunter College in New York. The author of many articles in psychiatric and psychoanalytic journals, he is a Fellow of the American Psychiatric Association and a practicing psychoanalyst in New York City.

Date Due